Twins: A

By Johnny Pearce

Twins: A Survival Guide for Dads.

Published by Ginger Prince Publications
Printed by Lightning Source International

Any views held by others in this book are not necessarily the views held by the author. The information provided in this book is not medical advice. For any advice on health issues, please refer to the relevant health practitioner.

Cover design: Ginger Prince Publications

Trade paperback ISBN:
978-0-9566948-4-3

GPP04

About the author:

Jonathan Pearce is a teacher from South Hampshire who has decided to try his hand at fathering twins. He's still alive, by all accounts, surviving on broken sleep and the cheeky laughs of his twin boys. His partner and the boys' grandparents enable him to get through the day in one piece and he owes them big time! He is an active philosopher and writer, as if he wasn't busy enough already.

When researching twins, he realised that there wasn't a book for dads out there. Now there is.

Acknowledgements:

I would like to take this opportunity to thank my partner Helen, whose patience and support have been legendary. She has also been a wonderful mother to our lovely twin boys, Finn and Oscar. In fact, without those two fantastic additions to our family, this book would not exist. A big thanks goes out to Karen Bleakley who read and reviewed the book from another parent of twin's perspective. Last but not least, I give a heartfelt appreciation of all the family and friends, grandparents and children, who have supported our two boys to the hilt, particularly Margaret and Ivan who have provided tremendous time and energy in helping us.

Dedicated to grandparents everywhere, particularly the boys' ones.

Thanks.

Contents

Introduction

As you sit in the darkened room, there is a sense of anticipation in the air. You know your other half is pregnant and has been for some thirteen weeks or so. The sonographer (which you have just found out is the person who operates the scanning equipment with a type of mystic genius that beggars belief) is moving her scanner around on your partner's basted stomach. Meanwhile, the screen dances to her deft touch; dark shadows, light grey clouds and white noise tango across the display in a mesmerising confusion. She is looking for a seven centimetre or so embryo. And finds it with consummate ease. Only, she says, "Well the good news is that this here," pointing at an image that looks like a cross between the most beautiful little thing you have ever seen, and an alien, "is baby. And this here, is another baby. Good news – you have twins."

Now, many things are presently rushing through your mind, a myriad of emotions and conversations with yourself, among which might well be:

- ☐ What wonderful news – the chance to bring two little lives into this world.
- ☐ Oh my God, I can barely afford to bring one child up, let alone two!
- ☐ Are they boy boy, girl girl, or boy girl? Will I be hopelessly outnumbered?

- ☐ As the captain of *Orpheus* in *Jaws* said, on catching the shark: "We're gonna need a bigger boat!" car / bedroom / house / holiday home in the South of France.
- ☐ AAAAARRRGGGHHH!
- ☐ All of the above

The emotions of the moment are to be savoured, and I hope they are pleasant, although everyone's situations are different. One thing is for sure, your life is never going to be the same again.

This book is designed to be a companion to the father-to-be of twins, helping him to understand the impact of impending twins on his life, helping him to understand what the other half is going through, and giving practical advice on everything from prams to breastfeeding (her, not you...).

As a first-time father of twins myself, this book will be a journey through the first few years of twin fatherhood, and a look at the years beyond that, with the aim of imparting some of that knowledge and useful advice to aid you, the reader. There are plenty of books out there to help the prospective parent of babies and twins, but so many of them are aimed at the mother. This is an attempt to redress the balance. Because, let's face it, a large majority of (first time) fathers don't know their arse from their elbow, their pram from their stroller, when it comes to babies. It's like being stuck in a jungle alone, when you've only ever lived in a flat in Peckham. Well this is your survival kit. Welcome to twins fatherhood: buckle up, it's a white knuckle ride.

PART I – PREGNANCY

Some facts and figures

Found below are a series of interesting facts that you can entertain your mates with down the pub, or break the ice with people at cocktail parties. Or read and forget within an hour. It's ok, keep the book on the bookshelf, and return to it when needed.

If you haven't experienced the early stages of pregnancy with a partner, or it's been so long that you have forgotten what it's all about, then let me enlighten you. As soon as you find out that you are having a multiple pregnancy, then I imagine you might start feeling like there are going to be more dates to organise, more equipment to buy, more facts to remember, and more things to worry about. The best thing to keep in mind is that you aren't the first couple to expect twins, and you certainly won't be the last. In the UK alone there are over 10,000 multiple births per year. Worldwide, twins make up almost 2% of the total population (there are over 125 million living multiples) whilst UK figures show that there are just over 15 multiple births (twins, triplets and higher) per 1,000 births, whereas the US has some 32 twin births per

1,000. The highest proportion of twin births is in the Yoruba ethnic community of West Africa, with 45 twin births per 1,000. They must be doing something funky. China, on the other hand, has the lowest, with 1 in every 300 births being multiple.

One term that will come out of the woodwork (you might wonder how it had by-passed your entire existence) is 'singleton'. Rather than being a small village in West Sussex, it actually refers to a single baby, as opposed to twins or triplets. Below are the expected pregnancy lengths for the respective birth types:

- Singletons 40 weeks
- Twins 37 weeks
- Triplets 34 weeks
- Quadruplets 32 weeks

So now you know how long you will have to massage your partner's feet for. Not continuously, of course. In all honestly, it goes on way beyond the birth of the babies... Their average birth weights are as follows:

- Singletons (see, there it is!) 3.5kg (about 7lbs 11oz)
- Twins 2.5kg (about 5lbs 8oz)
- Triplets 1.8kg (about 4lbs)
- Quadruplets 1.4kg (about 3lbs 1oz. Ooh that's small.)

It turns out that one third of all twins are identical, one third same sex fraternal, one third are girl/boy fraternal. Of the identical twins, half are boy/boy, half are girl/girl. The same is true of the same sex fraternal – a fifty/fifty split boy/boy and girl/girl. Twins also show a much higher tendency to be left handed – 22% of them as opposed to just under 10% in the general population. The average time between births of twins is 17 minutes. Although one doctor told us that the longest he had heard between the birth of twins was a whopping 106 days from a French woman, but in my research, the longest official one I could find was in the case of Mrs. Peggy Lynn who gave birth to Hanna on November 11 1995 and twin Eric on Feb 2 1996, 84 days later. That's a long labour...

The heaviest set of naturally-born, mixed-sex, UK twins weighed in at 18lbs and 3oz. Ouch. However, records show that the heaviest twins born were to Mrs. J.P. Haskin of Arkansas, on February 20 1924, totalling 27lbs 12oz. Yes, 27lbs 12oz. My goodness. That's alotta baby.

One amazingly 'virile' man was a Russian peasant named Kirilow who was presented to the empress of Russia in 1853 for his outstanding achievement: he had been married twice and his wives gave birth to 72 children including 4 sets of quads. 8 sets of triplets and 8 sets of twins. Sweet bejesus, that's alotta nappies.

Another nugget – cryptophasia, or idioglossi, is a language that some twins develop as their own (enter Mulder and Scully from the X-Files).

Vanishing Twins

Interestingly, there is much speculation in the realm of something called 'vanishing twins'. It is thought that a far larger proportion of conceptions were originally twins, to the tune of an estimated 1 in 8 births. That means that (while only 1 in 70 births actually produce twins) a vast amount of twin conceptions, thought to be anywhere from between 30% and 80%, result in the loss of one or both babies. Most of the time, these foetuses are reabsorbed without anyone knowing anything different. The phenomenon has only come to light in the advent of better ultrasound technology that highlights the twins in the first place. It gets more fascinating in regards to left-handedness. It has been hypothesised that left-handed people are actually mirror image identical twins where the right-handed twin has disappeared.

The how and why of twins

Many things can influence why a woman might conceive twins, and your partner might well have been affected by some of the following. A large influence is the maternal family history of twins. The chances of having twins increase four-fold if the mother is herself a fraternal twin. Other factors might be the mother's age, height or weight or race (or all four!). The father has absolutely no genetic influence on the chances of conceiving twins. Thus, twins will pass on the mother's side. Twinning rates seem to double for women over the age of 25

Increasingly, infertility or fertility issues have led to couples seeking fertility treatment. Increase in, and improvement of, IVF treatment has led to a rise in twin births. There are different procedures for different issues with regards to IVF, and it can depend on in which country you have the treatment carried out as to how many fertilised eggs are implanted. Often, two or more (outside of the UK) fertilised eggs are implanted into the mother, and if both of these take, then the chances of having twins increase. For example, if one egg is implanted, and the percentage chance of it developing are 33%, then the chances of having twins are low – the normal sort of rate associated with conception. However, if two eggs are implanted, and they both have a 33% chance of taking, then the overall chance of at least one taking is 66%. Hence why they implant two eggs. Using simple maths, we can see that the chance of twins, then, from both eggs taking is 33% - much higher than normal twin conception chances.

Identical twins, on the other hand, are not hereditary, and are thought to be little affected by any genetic factors. The rates around the world of identical twins are pretty much constant, irrespective of geography. Below, I will detail the different types of twins and how they come into being.

The different types of twins

Twins aren't just twins. There are different types of twins – different flavours with a myriad of labels. I will attempt to explain them all in layman's terms, equipped with a startling array of very simplistic diagrams. It may seem like an unnecessary amount of labels and science, but doctors and midwives *will* use these terms, and they will be liberally sprinkled on your partner's notes that she will have to carry around with her, so it is worth having the information to at least refer back to.

The female reproductive system produces the egg, or ovum, which, if fertilised by the man's sperm, becomes a zygote. This is the combination of the two genetic codes from mother and father. If this one zygote splits, then two identical twins form from the same set of cells. These twins are called monozygotic twins, developing from the one zygote, and representing about a third of all twins. It sounds obvious, but you'd be surprised at the amount of blokes that say "Oh yeah..." to this, but identical twins cannot be boy/girl. Which means that boy/girl twins cannot be monozygotic. Identical twins cannot be male/female but will always be the same sex.

About 25% of identical twins are known as 'mirror image twins', where if one is right-handed, the other is left handed; their hair will fall in opposite directions; their fingerprints are reversed; and other such characteristics.

On the other hand, sometimes a female may drop two eggs at the same time, and both these eggs can be fertilised from the same intercourse. When this happens, two separate zygotes are formed, and they will have different combinations of the parents' genes, and so will not be identical. These twins are called dizygotic or fraternal twins (di- being the prefix meaning two, hence two zygotes). 50% of these twins will be male/female. On very rare occasions, a woman can drop two eggs, and they can be fertilised by two different males. The twins are known as 'twins of two' and share 25% of their DNA with each other, being half-siblings. Another less frequent variety is the polar or half-identical twins. These twins arise when the female's egg splits *before* fertilisation and the two split eggs are fertilised by different sperm. They share 75% of their DNA.

So, that seems simple enough, no? Fraternal (non-identical, DZ or dizygotic) twins or identical (MZ or monozygotic) twins. These are the basic two types. However, the labels don't stop there since the way the twins develop in the womb, and the variety of egg sac combinations mean that one can get quite confused. Don't worry, keep this book on you, and revise in the clinic waiting room before seeing the doctor, and amaze him with your modern-man knowledge of all things pregnancy.

These two types of twin further develop into three types of twin. When the embryo starts developing, it does so within an amniotic sac, one of two membranes. The amniotic sac sits within another membrane known as the chorion. Your twins might well each sit within their own two membranes. These are called Dichorionic-Diamniotic (DiDi) twins. Check out my cheap diagram – the computer equivalent to drawing on the back of a beer mat.

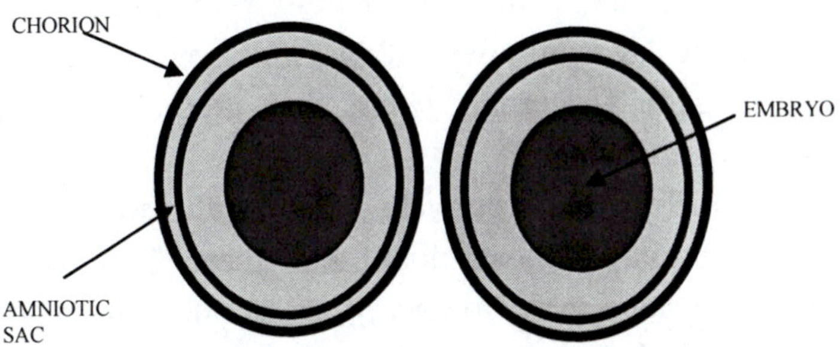

Dichorionic-Diamniotic (DiDi) twin embryos. Perhaps they look more like cartoon dogs' eyes...

This combination of sacs and membranes is the most common twin set up and has the lowest risk factor attached. The second variation is known as Monochorionic-Diamniotic (MoDi) twins. These twins share the outer membrane (chorion) but have their own amniotic sacs. See below for clarity.

Monochorionic-Diamniotic (MoDi) twins, all in one sleeping bag.

This type of twin occurs in 60-70% of monozygotic (when one egg splits) twins. DiDi twins occur in almost all dizygotic (fraternal) twins, and around 25% of monozygotic twins.

Finally, to complete the set, we have Monochorionic-Monoamniotic and these little ones share the same sacs. However, they do only have a 50-60% survival rate. Sharing the same placenta and sacs, these twins run the risk of having their umbilical cords tangled around each other, causing a range of complications.

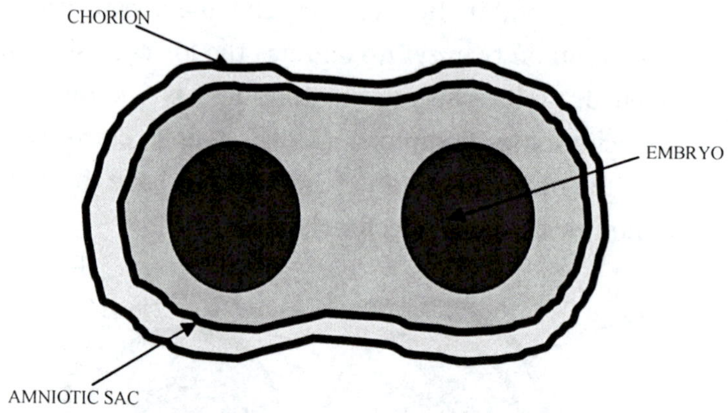

Monochorionic-Monoamniotic twin embryos. These ones involve the highest risk.

Scans and when she'll need them

It is important to note that scan procedures may well differ from hospital to hospital, so this will suffice as a rough guide. When you have found out that your partner is pregnant by demanding that she takes at least three pregnancy tests made by three different companies, and bought from three different chemists, your partner will need to speak to her doctor. Your doctor will book you in for an antenatal (before birth) appointment at around 10-14 weeks. The amount of scans that she will receive from then on will depend on what the hospital procedure is, but it will mainly vary due to the chorionicity. In other words, depending on what set up of embryos you have as mentioned in the previous section. Expect to be monitored to a much greater extent than a singleton pregnancy due to the fact that twin pregnancies are seen as 'higher risk'. Without wanting to scare you, the chances of complications are increased.

When sorting out your appointments, don't be afraid to be prepared by making lists of questions that you would like answered. This may normally be the sort of thing your partner does, but it might just pay to write a few things down. Ask about anything that you deem important, even if you think it might be stupid and obvious. You're a bloke, don't be afraid to sound like one at an antenatal appointment. Only your partner will laugh at you, and you only have to remind her of who'll be making her the tea over the next six months to stifle those chortles.

If you can get the time off work, or organise work to fit around your appointments, then I would definitely advise this. The few appointments that I missed, I was a little upset about – they are fascinating, interesting, and a good chance to bond with your partner over the upcoming challenges and joys. In most cases, you can have an extra person in with you to see the scans. My partner's mother and my mother were over the moon to be asked, and it really got them involved with the pregnancy, which is a vital thing, as you'll DEFINITELY be needing their help later on...

As many twin pregnancies these days are as a result of IVF (In Vitro Fertilisation), many readers of this book will have partners who may be having a scan at between 5 and 7 weeks of pregnancy. Modern ultrasound techniques and equipment means that you can tell this early whether your partner is carrying twins.

For non-IVF pregnancies, your first scan will be the dating scan at between 10 and 14 weeks. This may be doubled up with the nuchal translucency (NT) scan which has to be taken before 14 weeks. This scan is designed to screen your babies for chances of Down's

Syndrome. The normal screening procedure of a blood test at 16 weeks cannot be done with twin pregnancies. The NT scan measures the fluid at the back of the embryos' necks and has a 75% detection rate (though it only measures the chances, and a further test actually diagnoses Down's Syndrome).

The dating scan gives the length of your partner's pregnancy, which is calculated from the first day of her last menstrual period (LMP), even though she might not have actually conceived until 14 days after her LMP. The LMP is used because most women know when their last period was, but may not know when they actually conceived, especially if you have an active sex life, rather than on birthdays and at Christmas. Tell your partner not to have a wee before the dating scan, as the sonographer (the person that operates the machine that goes bleep) will need a full bladder to see things correctly. No, the sonographer won't need a full bladder, your partner will. Depending on the timing of the scan, the embryos will be around 3-7cm long from head to bottom.

We had a scan that seemed to cross all the 't's and dot all the 'i's at once. As well as dating and screening for Down's, the sonographer also did the chorionicity scan. This lets you know the set up of the placentas and membranes, and they can tell what type of twin combination you have as mentioned before. If both twins are sharing a placenta, this can lead to increased risk of complications. The pictures are great, and they will give you print-offs. We were even able to get a CD with quite a few photos and some video footage. Watching the little munchkins jump up and down with hiccups is a joy, and seeing your partners belly throw the foetuses around like an amusement park ride because you happened to crack a really bad gag at the time is also marvellous.

"What is a placenta?" I hear you ask in embarrassed confusion. Well, that's no great shakes, I'll explain simply. The baby grows in your partner's uterus (womb) and has an umbilical cord that connects it to the placenta. The placenta is attached to the uterine wall and allows blood and nutrients to be taken in and waste to be removed. Basically, the placenta represents the home counties, whilst the M25 represents the umbilical cord that connects London (the baby) to the rest of the country. London sucks the goodness out of the placenta and sends back wastage (commuter?) via the M25. Capiche?

After the scan(s) at around 14 weeks, you get a nice 6 week or so respite before having to go back in for the anomaly scan. This is to check to see if your embryos have... anomalies. The sonographer basically checks that your embryos are developing normally and that the placenta is lying in the uterus. This scan, in my opinion, is one of the best scans. Not only do you get, assuming good news, a clean bill of health (to a degree) for your twins, but also the quality of the scan is great. This is because the foetuses are small enough to both be clearly seen on the same scan, and yet big enough to be detailed and looking like real little babies. Later on in the pregnancy, the foetuses are often too big to be able to be seen clearly, and will rarely fit into a single scan together, like two little aliens in a small sack. To be able to make out their jaw bones and spines is a wonderful moment to share. They will give you print outs of this scan to add to your scrapbooks.

As with all of these scans, I am not in a position to give any advice to those who have bad news from any of them, since we were lucky enough to have had a textbook pregnancy. The hospitals and experts will provide all the treatment and advice in such eventualities.

The next scans will be in the third trimester. Pregnancy, for the uninitiated, is split into three trimesters, with each trimester being around three months. So after 6 months, your partner will be scanned more regularly. Twins being a 'high risk' pregnancy means that the professionals like to keep a close eye on proceedings. Part of the reason is because a midwife can't accurately feel the growth of two babies. Things can get a little squashed down there, and legs and arms and bodies bulge all over the shop, making midwives' endeavours that much harder. If your babies share a placenta you will need scans every fortnight, and if they have their own placenta, you are let off the hook with once every 4 weeks. Singletons don't get scanned at all at this stage, so count yourselves lucky (if you like your scans, that is)!

These scans are alternated with visits to see the consultant and midwife (separately) to talk about your various options. As a bloke, it is always worth trying to make these as to know as much as possible about what your partner will be going through, and to keep on top of things. Plus, you get to read lots of pointless women's magazines in the waiting rooms. There are an astonishing amount of crazy people out there who are willing to sell their insane stories for peanuts. You'll often pick up a magazine detailing some bizarre twins or even sextuplets story – enough to scare off the most comfortable of fathers-to-be...

Finding out the sexes

You will be given ample opportunity at each scan after 20 weeks to find out the sexes of each twin.

Singletons, if parents decide not to find out the sex, have no further scans after 20 weeks, and so cannot find out if they change their minds. With twins, there are plenty of opportunities if you change your minds. We decided to find out, and, wanting at least one boy, were really happy to be told we were expecting two boys.

The reasons that we wanted to find out were purely logistical, and I would give this as a salient piece of advice. Time is of the essence with twins, and the more organised that you can be before the births of your twins, the better. Whether it be painting the nursery / bedroom walls, or buying mountains of baby clothes, I really think it pays to know in advance for twins in a way that is not so necessary for singletons. It is amazing how much time twins require of you, compared to singletons, and painting an entire bedroom around looking after two newborns 24/7 is quite an ordeal. But then again, each to their own.

In our case, sexing was fairly easy due to the testicular endowment of the foetuses. Foetuses and newborns do generally have swollen and enlarged testicles which are quite evident to a trained sonographer. I was very surprised, though, to be watching the screen when the sonographer was trying to get the femur length of 'Twin 1'. Without zooming in or out, she moved up the foetus and showed what can only be described as a ghostly space hopper on the screen.

This entity was fully half the size of the femur. This was followed by guffaws and the predictable torrent of lines like "Ooh, he's just like his father" and "It's in the genes don't you know?" At least the sonographer laughed politely.

Finding out the sexes of the twins is also advantageous if your partner is due a baby shower, as I will now explain.

Baby showers

Baby showers are a relatively new thing in this country and have been a welcome invasion from the States. I say welcome because, quite frankly, everyone loves getting presents. A baby shower is a get-together of usually female friends, relatives and colleagues of the mum-to-be. Taking place at someone's house who can manage large amounts of wrapping paper, it pays for everyone to know the sexes up front so they can busy themselves with getting appropriate presents, rather than having to buy unisex clothing. That horrible yellow.

One of my colleagues at work who has a husband who she claims still lives in the early part of last century, after having his house volunteered as the party location, asked how it went. After learning that it was a success, he asked, "I've been wondering, how does the plumbing work for this new-fangled 'baby shower'?" Hmmm.

Now, to be perfectly mercenary about the whole thing, baby showers are great because having twins is an expensive occupation (yes, there are days when it feels like a job, and others when it feels like the greatest day you could have, but that's the case with any number of children). If there is an opportunity that you can get a large amount of baby stash, and especially since it will be new and not from *ebay*, then that opportunity must be grabbed with every available hand. We were hugely lucky to both be working in a school at the time, and so, with the predominance of female staff, mothers and associated school acquaintances, the baby shower was over-subscribed. And what a lovely array of presents we got. This valuable occasion allowed us to stock up, in advance, with vital supplies: clothing, toys, accessories, toiletries and suchlike. All of it welcome, and all of it subsequently used. And most of it can be *ebayed* after use! Everyone's a winner.

Equipment you'll need – being prepared

In this section I have listed a number of important things which I think you might need to think about before the birth of your little ones.

As the birth date gets closer and closer, and knowing the fact that there is a strong possibility that the twins can come early, there is a strong temptation to go out and buy as much stuff as possible in a retail frenzy. This frenzy isn't necessarily a bad thing. The world of baby shopping is a whole different experience then one you'll be used to. There are things that you can buy for babies that you never knew existed. In fact, you'll realise that babies have needs that you never knew existed. Having said that, there is an awful lot of stuff in baby shops and catalogues that I wager is completely unnecessary.

1. The car

So, what are the important things that need to be considered? More relevantly, what are the sorts of things that might be needed that a man like you would be interested in? I could bore you senseless with talk about breast pumps and nipple cream, but that would be dull. Let's talk about cars. That's a nice manly thing to do.

We were in a bizarre situation of only having a campervan, at the time, to get us about, so we wisely thought it might be time to invest in a car. But what car is ideal for twins? This is actually quite an important question, especially since there are many practicalities involved. For instance, with twins, you will need a buggy, and this will be considerably larger than the standard singleton buggy. As a result, whatever car you have, it is absolutely essential that you have a large boot. Otherwise, expect to be driving around with a buggy sticking out and a bungee cord keeping your car together! This then starts to put you into the realm of a people carrier, mini people carrier, or estate. Luckily, the popularity of people carriers has meant that the market has become saturated with different models to the point that they are fairly affordable, and the second hand market is never short of supply.

The other consideration is extra people. If you want to give two people a lift, and have yourself and your partner in the car, and your two twins (in car seats), then you will need a seven seater. We ended up getting a mini MPV (multi-purpose vehicle) in which the two back seats could be easily raised from the boot (a

Vauxhall Zafira, and I now understand why there are so many of them on the road). This type of car is much more handy than a full-sized MPV in which you can usually remove the two back seats altogether. However, you must consider that this will probably need to be done by your partner, if you are working, and those back seats in full-sized MPVs are incredibly cumbersome and heavy. Seats that pop up from the boot are very user-friendly indeed. Furthermore, the car will often be used for shopping trips, and with two adults and two children in seats, in a conventional car, it does not leave enough space for the shopping when you take into account a large buggy.

It is unfortunate that in this ecologically sensitive time, the best vehicles are the bigger ones, but then again, if they are too big, they can be unwieldy for the less confident driver, or for someone used to a smaller car. My partner has found our mini-MPV ideal and a real godsend. The days of being young and hip and having a sports car are over, or must be moved to days when you are given a green card. About once a year.

Whatever you buy, measure out the boot for the buggy. Or buy a buggy that fits your boot. If the two are incompatible, don't blame me if your neighbours complain about the language emitted from your driveway as you realise, on your first daytrip out, that your buggy is one inch too big for your boot.

Incidentally, we still have the campervan. It will be our holiday mechanism for the next five years. Twin babies on a plane? Possibly a little too stressful.

2. The buggy

I don't know if this is the same for every new father, but the first thing I do when I go into Mothercare is to check out the fine array of snazzy buggies arranged in tempting fashion at the back of the store. Move aside nappy cream, I wanna get my hands on something with wheels and clips, telescopic dooberries and foldable whatsits. And this, my friends, is a big decision. You see, there are two types of buggies to buy, and many pros and cons to weigh up. First of all, there is the tandem buggy, which has one seat sitting behind another. Alternatively, you can get a buggy where the seats sit side by side, usually called a twin buggy. I will set out the pros and cons into an easy to compare table for the literarily challenged:

	TWIN BUGGY	TANDEM BUGGY
ADVANTAGES	• Children sit next to each other and can interact with each other (later this can avoid arguments!) • Both children can see in front of them, interacting with their environment • Many different models, including 3-wheelers and all-terrain ones • Lighter than tandems	• Narrower, so good for getting through narrow doors, such as when shopping • Individual seats are usually a little wider than twin buggies
DISADVANTAGES	• Can be too wide for some doors • On some models, the seats can be quite narrow for when they are older	• Can be much heavier than twin buggies • Are generally less stable • More difficult to steer • Can be difficult to fold • One child looks into the back of another seat – not very interactive or interesting

Weighing up the pros and cons, we decided to opt for a twin buggy, mainly due to the fact that both children would be facing forward, and would be more stimulated. We made sure we got one that was 75cm in width so as to fit in standard doorways. Moreover, we got one that you could take the seats off and replace them with a double carrycot. We have had almost as many comments on our buggy as our children!

There is a plethora of makes and models, and it is a case of finding a style that suits you. We ended up becoming mildly obsessed with a New Zealand company called Mountain Buggy whose designs are robust and meant for all-terrain use.

These are very expensive brand new, as are many double buggies, and so we resorted to *ebay*, from which we got the buggy and a twin carrycot at knockdown prices (with a little patience as it is easy to get carried away on *ebay*!). The buggy is highly manoeuvrable, even with one hand, and Helen can even wheel it over the grass with ease to come and watch me play rugby. Nice.

As ever, find out the dimensions, measure your doors and your boot, and think about what the priorities are for you, since it will be the transport for your babies for the next few years, given that it is robust enough to last that long!

The carrycot that we had for our buggy was detachable, and acted as a pram when in transit, but could also be taken off and placed anywhere to allow the babies to sleep in when needed. In fact, they slept in the carrycot together as their bed for the first month. And my, they looked cute.

3. The cots

More decisions, but this time, I'm afraid, without wheels. What cots do you get them? The choice you have is whether to get one cot for them to sleep together in whilst you buy a bigger house / decorate a bigger room etc., or whether to get two cots straight up. Cots are not small things, and you will need two of them, eventually, and so finding the appropriately sized room is essential. Usually, cots will have either a drop side, or three levels to which you can set the mattress height, or both. This will mean that you do not have to break your back picking them up whilst they are young, by setting the mattress level nearer the top of the cot. You can also drop the side of the cot if you need to bend down and get the babies so as not to have to bend right over and into the cot. You'll be doing a lot of bending, so this is more useful than you might imagine!

We ended up settling for cotbeds. These are larger cots that can be rearranged to make small beds by removing the side bars and part of the ends. This means, as a long term investment, they can last until the children are around 5 years old. Again, being the penny-pinchers that we are, we opted for *ebay* and accepting a kind gift of my nephew's old cotbed. Thus, we ended up with two almost identical and very cheap / free cotbeds. We then bought the mattresses brand new from a reputable mattress dealer off, you guessed it, *ebay* (I should get commission...). Mattresses for cots are extortionate, they really are. Mothercare and other retailers will charge you £90 odd or more, and we got excellent, safe and well-made mattresses delivered for £30. A cotbed from a major retailer might cost you upwards of £130, and the mattress another £90. So for twins, that would be a minimum of £440. For our two cotbeds and brand new mattresses, we paid £110. It all helps!

But then again, if you are loaded and have much disposable income, then why not spank it up on a set of brand new cotbeds to fit in with the newly decorated designer nursery from the pages of *Ideal Home*!

4. Nappies

This may seem like the domain of your partner, but don't be put off – nappies can be exciting! Sort of. And what's more, you'll end up having poo as one of your main topics of conversation for the next three years. Most mothers seem to have a Pampers vs Huggies battle. But there is also the disposable vs re-usable issue. We like to think of ourselves as at least a little concerned for the environment. You see, disposable nappies cause local authorities a bit of a headache – some 3 billion, yes 3 billion, go to UK landfill every year. Nottinghamshire County Council, for example, claims it costs them £1 million a year. The average child will get through 6,500 nappies by the time they are two and a half – about 10 tonnes of waste. The environmental cost (carbon footprint, as well as all the chemicals needed to manufacture them) of making them and of them degrading is high. If you take the whole process of what it takes to create and dispose of disposable nappies, then re-usable ones are a fairly sensible option. Moreover, for twins, you would be looking, in that two and half year period of spending at least £2600 on disposable nappies, by my reckoning. Re-usables will save you many hundreds of pounds *at the very least*.

These days, re-usables are a completely different kettle of fish than even 5 years ago. The materials and ergonomics have been so much improved, that the absorbency and chances of leaking everywhere are far reduced. We spent out (they can seem expensive to buy new) on some really good UK manufactured re-usable nappies and were very happy with the result to begin with. With birth to potty models, you don't have to worry about getting different sizes – just adjust the poppers and Velcro. With enough of them, and a good system of washing and drying, it is definitely workable. In bigger cities, they even have schemes whereby people come round your house to pick up your re-usables, take them away to wash them, and bring them back clean. Aah, easy living.

However, we did find that after some time the nappies weren't able to keep the wee in for more than an hour and a half to two hours. I'm not sure whether it was the make of nappies or whether it was our boys being heavy wetters. That said, we didn't have the same problems with disposables. It meant that we used the real nappies when we didn't need to take the boys out but if we needed to leave the house, then we couldn't risk the real nappies. It is a shame since we really wanted to make them work.

For the first few weeks of our twins' newborn lives, we used disposables as they can be made to fit much smaller babies more adequately, and the amount of waste in our bins went up exponentially. Of course, they are not for everybody, and my partner took the first year off, and we do have help from her parents who come round to assist when they can. Horses for courses, and it depends what your priorities are. Really, the most important point to make is, don't let twins make you think that re-usables are too much. If you get the right ones, they can work for you.

Easy living + landfill = disposables

A bit of effort + smug contentment = re-usables

5. Car seats

Don't forget to get hold of two car seats early doors or you'll be in Argos when she's giving birth! Car seats are obviously, and legally, vital. They come in various sizes depending on what size and age the babies are. The smallest size for newborns, which is what you will need, is Group 0 (or Stage 1), and they are called infant carriers. Below is a chart that might come in handy:

Weight range	Approximate age suitability	Group
From birth to 10kg (22lb)	Newborn to nine months	0
From birth to 13kg (29lb)	Newborn to five to 18 months	0+
9kg to 18kg (20lb to 40lb)	Nine months to four years	1
15kg to 25kg (33lb to 55lb)	Up to six years	2
22kg to 36kg (48lb to 79lb)	Up to 12 years	3

Group 0 are the lay-down variety that can also be attached to certain models of compatible buggies, which can be very useful. These are known as 'travel systems'. Infant carriers are not designed to be used in the front seats of cars that have airbags. The carriers are rear-facing and airbags are more danger than good to these car seats, and the babies they are carrying.

Yet again, with the cost of twins in easy reach of spiralling to vast sums, we took to begging and borrowing. As long as car seats have not had any bumps, they are perfectly safe to use second hand. Because we both work in a primary school, we were offered all sorts of clothing and gear. And we have ended up with three infant carriers, and five other seats of varying stages. Hundreds of pounds worth of goods that we will, in turn, pass on.

Shops such as Mothercare have a wide variety of seats, and have staff trained especially in car seat knowledge. If you have money to burn, the choice of brand new stuff at retailers is sometimes overwhelming. There is a theory, called the Paradox of Choice, where if you have too many items to choose from, it stuns you and it is harder to make the final choice. Sometimes I feel that paradox when stumbling around a big Mothercare or Babies 'R' Us, mesmerised at the sheer quantity of choice of things I never knew existed!

Again, needing two of everything makes things more expensive, and means that you need a bigger car / room / house for the mountains of equipment.

6. Baby clothes / accessories / stuff

Leave it to the missus. You'll only buy the wrong size or colour. Or you'll get a cheap manual one, and she'll want a swanky electric one (or vice versa). Trust me, these things are her domain. Just accompany her, nod, smile and say "Yes sweetheart, they'll look adorable in that".

7. A bag to take to the hospital

If you are holding to gender stereotypes, then your partner will surely have packed her bag in organised expectation of the coming births. Probably at around ten weeks of pregnancy. And you'd better start thinking about it too! The nature of twins is that they are fairly likely to be born premature, and sometimes, very premature. As a result, a sensible couple will have their bags packed as early as possible to avoid a manic scramble, and a half-packed bag of nonsense in the event of a premature rush to the maternity unit.

So what do you need? The list that I will give you is based on the fact that you could be waiting around the hospital for some time, and they aren't the most exciting of places to hang out, generally being full of people with problems. No one goes to a hospital to receive a present for being really healthy, or because they have a particularly healthy pair of legs. No, it's usually cancer this, tumour that, amputation this and floppy that. The only real joy you get out of hospitals are maternity units, and breast augmentation theatres...

Anyway, back to the subject in hand, what to pack? If you're quick enough, then you can be supportive and help pack her bag, finally mastering how women fit so much stuff in their handbags. Below is a handy table / checklist to ensure that both you and your lady are at least a little prepared for the oncoming rush, panic and welcoming of two little heads into the world:

Her bag	Your bag
Loose, comfortable clothes that she'll love lying around in (painfully) and that she doesn't mind getting a little mucky.	Clothes, and some spare pants, t-shirt and socks if you're in for the long haul.
Dressing gown	ipod
Mobile phone and charger	Mobile phone and charger
Slippers	Good book
Massive maternity pants	Magazines
Nursing tops for breastfeeding	Money for car parking fees – nothing's for free these days. Make sure you have

	about £10 in coins saved up.
Something tip-top to wear on the way home – it's a special outing.	Camera and spare batteries – you don't want to have a useless camera at the key moment.
Toiletries	Toiletries
Toothbrush/paste	Toothbrush/paste
Maternity sanitary towels	Travel or electronic games
Newborn nappies – possibly the very smallest size if they are premature.	Snack foods
Nappy sacks	High energy drink
Bowl for water and cotton wool (or baby wipes, though they say that cotton wool is better for the skin)	Watch with seconds to time contractions
2 blankets	
2 best newborn clothes for their big return home	
Other baby grows and clothes (jackets, vests, snowsuits etc.)	
Booties and hats	
Maternity notes	

The other key thing to remember is try to keep the car full, or not near empty, with fuel. It's important to remember, at the beginning of the pregnancy, to keep the calendar free at around the time of the due date. No weddings or stag dos over those weekends, because you really need to be on hand at any moment. It's no good being three sheets to the wind with your mates in Bristol at a lapdancing club on a stag do whilst your partner is contracting at a rate of knots in the suburbs of Huddersfield. You won't be flavour of the month. Ever.

As mentioned in the table, make sure that the maternity notes are to hand – these are pretty vital. If you're new to the area, or not near your home, then find out where the hospital is in advance, and get to know the route – set that destination as a favourite in your Sat Nav. Hospitals can be confusing and massive complexes, so doing a dry run can be wise to find out where to park and where to drop off, and whether there are roadworks and suchlike.

Another crucial must-do: you really need to fix both car seats in the back of the car. If they are not fixed in, make sure you know how to do it! Practice a few times, so you're not fumbling around in the freezing cold with two little babies screaming because their Daddy doesn't know his arse from his elbow. Not everyone drives, of course, and if this is the case for you, then make sure you have your driver at a moment's call, or a taxi number to hand (and sort out car seats for them, too). Oh, and if you're a Londoner, don't forget to sort out the congestion charge if you're passing through those pesky zones.

When you're driving (and remember, you *should* be driving, and *not* calling 999), don't charge around like a lunatic, you'll just make things worse. Take it easy, there should be plenty of time. Normally.

You know it's time to go to the hospital when:

- The flood-gates open and the waters rush out.
- Your partner's contractions are strong and regular, lasting around a minute and occurring around every five minutes.

PART II – THE BIRTH

What type to birth to opt for

Births come in all shapes and sizes, and you will be offered several options as to how your partner would like to give birth to your twins. The most obvious and natural method is a VB – a vaginal birth (not an Australian beer). I will come back to this later.

The second option is a Caesarean birth, which involves cutting a line across the tummy and making a sun roof and ejecting the babies from there. A Caesarean incision for twins is slightly longer than for a singleton. Many consultants will press for a Caesarean (particularly if it a birth to an older mother), but most midwives will tell you that VBs are the way to go if the babies are in the right position. With twins that are in the same amniotic sac, things are a little more complicated, and a Caesarean will normally be insisted upon. However, with DiDi twins (different amniotic sacs and different chorions), we found that we were still mildly pressured to opt for a Caesarean. This is because, with twins being a higher risk pregnancy, the consultants like to feel they have as much control as possible over proceedings. Caesareans give them this control, as the birth is performed on their terms. However, if the babies are in prime positions, then there is nothing to stop you going for a vaginal birth. In fact, midwives are now trying to persuade more mothers to opt for natural births as they are, well, more natural. And probably cheaper.

So what's all this about baby positions? Surely they can come out any old how? Well, they probably could, but that's not ideal. For VBs, ideally both babies should have their heads pointing down, aiming for the real world like a torpedo. This is known as being cephalic (a cephalic presentation). If a baby is lying feet first or buttocks first, this is known as breech. If both babies are breech, then you'll end up having a Caesarean. If one is breech, and the other cephalic, then it depends which twin is doing what. Twin 1, the one who is closest to the cervix and will come out first, defines the situation here. If Twin 1 is breech, then a Caesarean will result, but if Twin 1 is cephalic and Twin 2 is breech, they *can* get Twin 1 out naturally, and move Twin 2 around inside to a better position. In our case, Twin 1 was cephalic, and Twin 2 was transverse (sort of crossways) until nearer the date when they both opted for cephalic, which was nice. However, they didn't seem to want to come out, so we had to lump for an induction.

Induction

If your partner hangs on for the full 38 weeks, which is statistically less likely, then you will be hauled in for an induction. This can be a very frustrating state of affairs if labour wards are busy. We were on the end of a phone for several days waiting to be allowed into the labour ward. Pregnancy rates were soaring in our local hospital and, as mentioned, inductions are low down the priority list. Luckily for me, as a teacher, I was on holiday and so there were no logistical ramifications. However, had I been working, or in a different job, things could have got really tricky. What made matters worse is that when we finally did get into the hospital, Helen had to wait in the antenatal ward for a day with seven other women, waiting for a lull in proceedings to allow for a clearance in the backlog of inductions.

The twins didn't help themselves either, as they refused to make a showing, and Helen was plied with various drugs to bring along the induction. This started with pessaries. Yes, up there. These dilated the cervix (the bottleneck above the vagina that is pinched closed, keeping the babies in the womb) enough for her waters to be broken, but the contractions did not follow with enough oomph to get things moving. Consequently, Helen was put on some drugs through an IV drip.

Unfortunately the drip had no effect either, and as her waters had been broken some time before, we had no option but to go for a 'planned' C-Section. It had been a long time coming!

What to do first

Assuming none of the above ... Aaaarrrrggh, it's happening! Don't panic, it's all been done before. A lot. If you are already a father, there's a lot that will be the same. If your partner's waters break, then you'll be off to the hospital fairly sharpish. As soon as labour starts (as soon as your partner starts having contractions) you should phone the labour suite and ask for advice. With twins, no one likes to take risks, and so advice is always to stay on the safe side.

In our situation, my partner Helen went full term, which in the case of twins, is 37-38 weeks. At this point, doctors will elect to induce the babies if they haven't already jumped out. Induction can be a bit of a bother because more urgent 'natural' pregnancies take priority, as seen in the previous section.

Let us start with a natural vaginal birth. Assuming everything goes to plan, and your partner is contracting, when you get to the labour ward a midwife will look after her in a private room. Pulse and blood pressure will be taken, followed by a good feel to see where the babies are positioned. This will be followed by an internal examination to see the state of the cervix giving a good indication of how far along she is. In a VB, these checks will happen with good regularity. With twin births, both twins are constantly connected to heart monitors, so that there is a constant record of how they are doing. These heart monitors are sensor pads strapped around your partner's belly in the right place to gauge the babies' heart beats, and often need to be moved and adjusted as the babies dance around the womb.

Many couples like to have birth plans so that they know exactly where they are during the birth. These plans set out what preferences they have, what support they would like, what procedures and drugs they may or may not want. Personally, we did not see much of a point in a birth plan; these are possibly things that are attractive to those who can't get through a day without writing at least three lists. Essentially, if you need something, or have any ideas on how you want the birth to go, simply let the midwife know as they are generally very accommodating. Midwives are founts of knowledge and advice and are generally very helpful indeed. Most of them have been through every type of birth, they've been there and done that, so use them and listen to them.

This first stage of labour will be very much like a singleton labour, other than the fact your partner will have two heart monitors attached and will receive more regular check-ups. Strong contractions should indicate a cervix getting itself ready and opening. It's always wise now to do anything that your partner wants from massaging and rubbing to going to the shop to get her anything she wants. Women react in very different ways from wanting you close and helping out in any way, to swearing at you and wanting you expletively out of her sight! You'll have to do your best to make yourself indispensible.

Some midwives advise a twin mother to try sitting forward over the back of a chair, or leaning over the table. These positions are known as 'optimal foetal positioning'. The theory is that the position allows for optimal space so that the babies can turn and move if needs be. Some people even advise doing this through the last trimester of pregnancy, too.

Pain relief

You and your partner will have discussed pain relief beforehand and it may well be the central basis of your birth plan. Gas and air (Entonox) is the most common pain reliever, and is on hand to be taken as often as is necessary without any lasting effects. Go on, have a go yourself. If this is not enough, pethidine can be injected. This is a little more controversial due to the fact that it can cause the babies to be slower and less responsive and can cause general dizziness.

Many people use TENS machines to help control the pain. These little machines send electric currents into the body which inspire the body to release its own natural painkillers. The current is adjustable, so expect it to be switched onto 11 out of 10. Don't worry, it's not quite electro-shock therapy.

The famous epidural is another option. Epidurals split people in two. Not literally. But many people swear by them and many people are a little distrusting of a needle injected into the spine. However, epidurals are safe, though there is always a (very small) risk involved with anything to do with the spine. Epidurals mean that there is no pain sensation and the birth is a pain-free process. Your partner will be numb from the waist down which can be an odd sensation. However, this can mean a longer labour as she will not be able to feel many things. As a result, pushing can be a more difficult process. With twins, many consultants advise epidurals, but it is by no means necessary. We were strongly advised by one consultant but allowed to freely choose natural birth by another; it depends who you talk to. The epidural can be topped-up as its effects wear off if the labour is dragging on.

Another option is a spinal injection. This is not to be confused with an epidural. It works faster than an epidural and is administered to the small of the back where it gets to work numbing the nerves that supply the womb and the cervix (the bottleneck keeping the baby in). These are single injections as opposed to the epidural which leaves a tube in the back to allow for further top-ups, and they can only be given once. The side-effects are minimal – occasional itchiness and headache.

The second stage

The first stage is where the cervix is opening enough for the baby to want to come out. There shouldn't be any pushing in the first stage, although the contractions can inspire some guttural grunting or choice language.

The second stage is action stations. Assuming the natural birth here, your partner will have been hooked up to two heart monitors and a consultant or midwife will have been checking for how much the cervix has dilated – how much the bottleneck has widened ready for the two wide-load vehicles to come through the tunnel. When she is dilated enough, your partner and yourself will be moved from the labour ward to the birth ward where no doubt you will hear grunts and screams of pitched pregnancy battles. You will generally have quite a few hospital experts hanging around now as twins are slightly more risky. For example, you might have three midwives, two obstetricians, two paediatricians, two resuscitation units and two cots in the room.

The midwife might try your partner in different positions to help the birth or to ease pain. It will be even harder for your partner to negotiate her movements if she is near full term with double the load. Remember to stay as encouraging as possible throughout the whole labour and birth period, despite the choice home truths she is screaming at you. If both babies are cephalic (head down), then things should be fine. Messy, but fine.

The pushing is a painful ordeal, apparently. "You've never experienced the pain of childbirth!" is something that you'll have held over you for an eternity. However, you have a fine rebuttal to that accusation since no woman has ever experienced the sheer terror and torture of man-flu.

Once the head of the first twin crowns, you're in business. Some more grunting and pushing and you'll have the first of two little cherubs, albeit pretty messy. Amongst the blood and white 'vermix' substance you'll have a baby! Check your watch and remember that time, and then clear the tears from your eyes, whilst complaining about dust particles or the light. Once the baby is out, the umbilical cord will be severed and the baby will be thankfully cleaned up and weighed, and a vitamin K jab administered (not one of the ones usually added to your cornflakes). Give baby a hug and start getting used to the crying! Of course, you might also be taking pictures or filming. Don't forget to ask someone to take some of you, too.

However, all is not over since you have a second one to come out. This can take anything from fifteen minutes onwards. Once your second comes out, and they clean and weigh, then your journey will almost be over. Almost.

If the first or second baby is feeling too comfortable inside to want to come out, they may use forceps or a ventouse (a vacuum device) to help get them out.

The third stage of the birth comes next. With some added pushing, the placentas will be pushed out. This can take longer than you might think or hope for. The team will usually show you the placentas for the sake of interest. Hmmm, nice.

By examining the placenta, they can usually tell if your twins are identical or not and failing that, you may be able to ask for blood tests on the umbilical cords. DNA tests can also be done on cheek swabs.

With the two little bundles of life now safely (hopefully) into the world, it is time to take a deep breath, wipe away the tears and think about texting the whole world. It's also the time to decide which twin gets which name. We had decided to call ours Oscar and Harvey, but neither looked like a Harvey, so we changed on the spot to Finn and Oscar (Oscar got Harvey as a middle name). Don't worry, though, as you have up to six weeks to name them!

You are now the proud dad of twins. Good effort.

Caesarean Section

Many twin births will either be a pre-arranged C-Section or an 'emergency' one. The emergency one may not be, in the common parlance use, a 'real' emergency (only about 6% are real emergencies), but a situation where they decide that the birth is no longer viable naturally, and so your partner may be whipped off to the theatre for an unplanned C-Section. The difference between this and a planned C-Section can be the access to the drugs available for painkilling. Being prepared and under no time pressures for a planned C-Section can help produce a calmer and more expected atmosphere. Sadly, in emergency C-Sections, no birthing partners are usually allowed.

C-Sections are actually quite major operations, which can be forgotten in the light of how common they are. As a result, you will have to be properly attired. You will have to wear blue cotton theatre clothes and special rubber shoes, mask and hat. Your partner will be on a drip and be given a regional anaesthetic to numb the area they cut. Effectively, they will be performing an aerial extraction from your partner's uterus to evacuate the hostages. Your partner will also be given the one article all lazy men have dreamed of – a catheter. This will mean, since she will be losing all sensation and will be unable to hold her bladder, that she can urinate freely and without worry.

Machines that go *ping!* will be monitoring her heart rate and blood pressure. A screen will be put up over your partner's chest so both of you are shielded from the delights of major surgery. The doctor will cut horizontally across the lower belly. Some tissue and muscle will be cut, but the major muscles of the tummy are moved aside, as is the bladder, to access the womb. Just as with a natural birth, the lower twin is born first, and then the higher one. The procedures for the babies afterwards are the same.

The umbilical cords will be cut and fastened about a couple of inches from where the belly button will be. These pieces of cord will eventually go black and will drop off several days later. Something to stick in your scrap books...

With C-Sections, the birth is the quick bit. Anyone can rip a hole in a piece of cloth. It's the sewing back up that takes all the time! The cut will be stitched or stapled together. These days the operations are very well carried out and the scars generally heal very well and with minimal issue.

For those mothers who want to breastfeed, once they are stitched up and in the recovery room, now's the time. Get them latched on early, that's the hope. This is something I will return to soon, as it has a massive impact on the life of the father.

Handy Hints for dads in labour

No, not dads in labour themselves (despite what you've read in those women's magazines)! Whilst I have given a few hints on what to do in the event of your partner going into labour, it will be useful to sum up the dos and don'ts into one handy section.

You must remember that the labour is all about the mother. You are effectively superfluous to requirements. As a result, you have to *make* yourself needed. Be useful. Be organised. Know what has been packed and where everything is. When your partner screams, "Get me my tissues!" you know exactly where they are and can efficiently find and supply them. This includes having enough car park change and enough money to buy whatever is demanded from the hospital shop. But only that, but you might need to take yourself away for a much earned tea-break and bacon sandwich – all of which requires money.

You need to be as positive and reassuring as possible. Help your partner through the tough times and tell her how well she is doing, no matter how you feel and in as relaxing a manner as you can.

As well as being as positive as possible, you also need to pander to her every need. This means doing what she, or any member of staff, ask of you.

Now, many will advise you not to be a nuisance and to stay out of people's way, whether it be your partner or the staff. I would agree with this though did not practice what I preach. I thought it was a good idea to try to be a comedy genius in the labour ward, giving a running commentary and generally making a nuisance of myself. It's a fine line between funny and annoying, evidently.

Ways to be useful might be to time the contractions (how long they lasted and how long between each contraction). When she is in great pain, you must be the one to help her through her breathing: breathe with her whilst looking into her eyes and holding her hands. Of course, if you are not a tactile person then she might be taken aback. Could be Brownie points in the bag.

The babies are born

So you have two new babies. Wow, what a rush! Two entirely new lives dependent upon you and your partner. And if your partner has had a Caesarean, then those babies are counting on you. This is because C-sections require a much longer time to recover from. Your partner will be feeling pain and discomfort with any kind of movement, even coughing and laughing. My exceptionally funny jokes became even more painful to Helen than they usually are. You should be on call to help her to move as necessary.

Usually after a C-section, your partner will spend three or four days in hospital, though you can leave after 24 hours (as Helen did). The recovery period lasts some time and doctors advise not driving for up to six weeks after the operation. Check with your insurance company that your partner is insured to drive if she does go for it early doors. Unluckily, such a lengthy recovery means that you may well have to do the vacuuming and the ironing. Hard luck, soldier.

In this recovery period, if your partner has a particularly painful wound to heal, then you will be needed to be the primary carer for the twins. This is no mean feat. If they are your first, you will no doubt have to learn how to put a nappy on (the baby, not yourself).

Of course, there are not only two of them to put nappies on, but being twins, they might well be very delicate and small. This is quite a skill. Luckily enough, as I will mention soon, they will spend much time sleeping and also feeding.

Premature twins

A 2008 TAMBA survey reported that only 43% of twin pregnancies and 1.5% of triplet pregnancies lasted over 37 weeks. This means that the majority of twin births are, to varying degrees, premature. Factors that contribute to premature births are previous premature births, poor diet, diabetes, smoking, and of course twin and multiple births. If you are pregnant with twins or multiples, then you are simply fighting a statistical full-term battle in the hope of getting to 38 weeks.

Usually, if your babies are born before 35 weeks, they will be admitted to the neonatal intensive care unit (NICU), and after 35 weeks, to the special care baby unit (SCBU). In the same TAMBA survey, 44% of mothers of twins said that at least one of their babies received support from an NICU. Over half of all twin babies and 99% of triplet babies weighed below 2.5kg (5lb 8oz) at birth. The NICU will give your babies 24-hour care, but it may be a few days until you or the mother can see them. In some cases, the father, being more active, will be able to see them first. Often, the unit will have instant cameras so that you can take some pictures to show your bed-stricken partner. There are lots of machines and procedures and it can be a very stressful time for parents. You will only be allowed reduced access and ability to touch, hold and feed them after they are healthy enough.

Due to being evacuated early, premature babies look thinner with less fat on them and still have a layer of dark hair, or lanugo which should soon disappear.

I won't go into the details but the support needed to breathe, receive enough nutrients, keep them from catching ailments and so on is understandably huge. The units around the country do a wonderful job in nursing premature babies to full health. It might well be worth visiting your local NICU before the birth of your babies to familiarise yourself with the unit and better understand the care provided, since there is a fairly good chance you'll be back there.

Research shows that premature babies really thrive on skin-to-skin contact, or kangaroo care as it is referred to. Your partner will also need to pump milk as much as possible. Her expressed breast milk will be a vital ingredient in giving your babies all the right nutrients and health benefits. The smell and sound of the mothers (and fathers) will be of comfort.

Because of all the strict timetabling necessary in neonatal care units, parents of premature twins are often in a good position to continue a routine. This can be really beneficial for your little ones. Your support, as well as support from family and friends will be vital for both the babies and your partner. There are many good sources for support, such as TAMBA (Twins And Multiple Births Association) and BLISS (the premature baby charity) who can offer sound advice and support for parents with premature babies.

Having said all this, since my experience has not been with premature babies, it would be a little presumptuous to provide an overlong piece of guidance for parents with premature babies. I'll leave that to the experts.

Recovery time in hospital

If your partner has had a C-Section or a particularly tough natural birth, then there might well be an extended stay for her in hospital. Given that your twins will still be at hospital, these may well be the quietest nights' sleep for the next twenty years if the excitement of being a new father to twins doesn't keep you up. That said, you will no doubt have been given a list of things to do and buy for your partner. There'll be a lot of rushing around before getting back to hospital to help out as soon as possible and see those little newborns.

You might, if you are technologically literate, want to take this opportunity to use you mobile or facebook account to spread more detailed news and pictures of the newborns to expectant family and friends on all corners of the globe. Modern technology makes the sharing of these wonderful moments so much easier.

Top ten things that annoyed the hell out of me

1. Baby-wipes that don't separate when they come out of the pack. Sheesh. When you have one hand holding baby's legs back, and one hand to pull the baby-wipe (singular) out, you don't, I repeat, don't want seven wipes coming out in one long line. And then having to shake them with

your one hand and seeing them fly everywhere. And yes, I did write an email of complaint to the most prominent manufacturer of said wipes. And yes, they did give me a £10 voucher. And no, they probably won't pass it on to their design team. Look, the design criteria is to have a good, cleansing wipe which comes out of the packet and detaches from the next wipe. Easy, eh? Wrong. I need to get over this.

2. Poppers. Certain configurations of poppers on babygrows and other pieces of clothing will annoy you. Why don't they put the poppers in the same place as that other babygrow? They will annoy you even more if your babies, like ours, are hyperactive. Trying to pop all the poppers on a screaming, squirming bundle of legs and arms is very frustrating. Take a deep breath.

3. Buttons. Why not poppers?

4. Surely not another popper rant? Er, sorry, but yes. If you have a wriggler, like we do; if you have a baby who hates being on their back; if you have a baby who hates having their nappy changed; if you have a baby who goes nuts when being forced to do something he has no inclination to do, then trying to put a nappy on them, and

worse still, trying to do their poppers up is a complete nightmare. It might even take two of you: one to pin them down, the other to pop poppers under pressure. Oh, to reason with a baby!

5. Furniture nuts and bolts on cotbeds that need adjusting. And having to do two sets of them

6. Nappies. Nappies are fine. Unless you have one twin who hates lying on their back, and thus hates having a nappy put on them more than anything in the world. Then they aren't so fun.

7. Newborn baby seats not being compatible with lap-belts so that I could only take one newborn twin in my campervan (it's too old to have an airbag).

8. Sleep deprivation. Enough said.

9. Shops that fill their stores with so much crap that negotiating a twin buggy is very difficult. It makes you wonder whether they are actually wheelchair friendly!

10. Parents (and their children) who tell you that their babies slept through the night from the age of 8 weeks. Gits.

PART III – THE FIRST YEARS

Those first few weeks

The freight train that are your twins will now be hitting you full on. Your life will change. Some of it won't be easy, either (I won't lie), but it is all worth it, believe me. Time to yourself and yourselves will now be timetabled and rare. Doing your own things which interest you will take a back seat. And no, you can't have a lie-in. Tough.

So you and your partner are now home, and the twins are with you. They may have been naturally born and gone full term, or may have had an extended visit to various units to nurse them to respectable 'birth weights'. Either way, your home is now shared with two complete dependents. And they depend on you. It is around now that you will be figuring out, as you go along, exactly what you forgot to buy, and what you never got round to doing or fixing.

If you had a baby shower, then you may well have a plethora of baby toiletries that will keep you going for years. I know we received enough baby lotion and baby shampoo to bathe a small European nation (So, how many things can you use baby lotion for? Hair product? Milk substitute for your cornflakes? Engine lubricant?).

At this early stage, any help that you can be given by friends and family is most welcome. Whether it be parents (-in-law), older siblings of the twins, neighbours or whoever, help with cooking and cleaning and all the things you take for granted as normally being able to do is great.

Hopefully, you have made sure that you have enough newborn-, or premature-sized baby clothes. You can never have enough vests.

Routine

Even at this age, and perhaps particularly, a routine is really important. And not only for the babies, but also for you. It is really valuable to know what you need to be doing and when. With so little time to yourself compared to what you are used to, it is great to be organised and to be working to a timetable. Now, for someone like me (disorganised, tardy, no routine) this can come as a shock, but a welcome shock. Moreover, you will actually find, believe it or not, that as the children become progressively older and bigger, you will have even less time to yourself. You see, when your babies are newborn, they spend a greater portion of the day sleeping.

Sleep

It is important to note that all children differ and some children need more sleep than others, whilst some children might need less. Also, with twins, you might have two different sleeping requirements for each of your babies. This can be a little trying as it gets your children out of synch, so attempting to get their sleeping habits in synch might be advisable.

Babies need a lot of sleep in the early stages; however, not for very long with each cycle. This means that *your* sleep will not be for very long and might well be often interrupted. Your babies' brains will be changing much, and most of this is done during REM sleep, which is the lighter form of sleep.

After maybe six to eight weeks, your babies will start sleeping for shorter periods in the day and for longer periods at night. If you are super lucky, your babies might even begin to sleep through the night after two months. I hate parents who told me that theirs did.

Ours didn't start sleeping through the night until after reaching a year old.

Although, strictly speaking, your babies won't start developing sleep habits until they are six weeks old, it is useful to try to get into habits early. You or your partner will start to understand the sleeping rhythms of your children and will see the signs that they are tired.

I would advise, certainly for the first few months, putting the twins in your room so that you can bond and keep a good eye on them through the night. We found that two cotbeds were ideal, and put them both in one cotbed in our room. First of all, they slept side by side, and then toe-to-toe before finally outgrowing the one cotbed for the two of them, and moving into their own room with the two cotbeds. Early on, your twins will be comforted by being in close contact with each other. This was also a comfort for my partner! However, do not do this in a smaller crib or Moses basket as they can overheat. When they can roll over, it is then that you want to move them to separate cots.

Sleep deprivation for you will be one of your biggest challenges over the next year. Fact. Nothing quite compares to the lack of sleep you will suffer, and you need to be wary of this depending on what job you do. It might have greater repercussions if you drive a lot or operate heavy machinery compared to if you work in the corner of an office.

Age	Night-time Sleep	Daytime Sleep	Total Sleep
1 month	8½	7(3 naps)	15½
3 months	10	5 (3 naps)	15
6 months	11	3¼ (2 naps)	14¼
9 months	11	3 (2 naps)	14
12 months	11¼	2½ (2 naps)	13¾
18 months	11¼	2¼ (1 nap)	13½
2 years	11	2 (1 nap)	13
3 years	10½	1½ (1 nap)	12

A table showing average sleep needed for the various ages of your babies.[1]

However, it does get better, believe me. For the first few months for us, they woke up every 2-3 hours for

[1]http://www.babycentre.co.uk/baby/sleep/sleepneeded/ retrieved 09/08/2011

feeds. Helen was breastfeeding them, and I will talk about this in the next section. I usually woke up with her, and thus both our sleep was interrupted, though hers more than mine. After the first few months, they always seemed to, after being put down at 18:30, wake up at around 21:30 and then several times throughout the night. Between six and eleven months, they woke at 21:30 and then again at around 11-12pm, and then another time in the night. At around 11 months, if we were lucky, after being put down at 19-19:30, they would wake up at 11-12pm and then sleep through. Awesome. But there were also bad nights, when they just wanted feeding or comforting much more.

An important strategy for twins is to put them down (no, not inject them with lethal doses of sedative) at the same time. This will help to synchronise them, though one may scream a little to start with. I have found it amazing that most twins (ours included) become immune to each other's crying and screaming, particularly when they are younger. One baby can be screaming their head off, and the other, lying right next to them, is soundly asleep. Of course, if yours don't form this selective deafness, then you will have a difficult time with your twins waking each other up consistently.

Some twin parents prefer to let their twins develop individual approaches to sleep routines. If this is the path for you, then make sure you start it early.

Also, try to put them down before they are actually asleep. This is something Helen was hot on as it helps them learn to sleep alone and associates sleep with their bed / cot. It also ensures that they won't be surprised about where they are when they wake up, since it will be the same place as when they fell asleep.

Now, some really important advice. When it is night time, try not to play or encourage your babies to think it is anything other than a quiet time. You need to teach your babies that night time is night time and sleep time. This can be really difficult when your babies are unbearably cute and demand cuddling and playing with, poking in the ribs, and tickling to raucous laughter. This is even more difficult if you work late and don't get home until after or near when they go to bed. As hard as it is, you cannot encourage them to play with you when it is 'night time'. Honestly, it will come back and bite you on the arse further down the line.

If your babies are struggling to get to sleep, it is often worth trying to swaddle them with blankets quite tightly. They seem to like this and it really helps to get them off to sleep.

Moses baskets, cribs, bouncy chairs and any other number of jiggable things might also help to rock those little ones off to sleep. It's also wise to make sure that your babies are warm, but not too warm. Getting it just right is really important.

The golden question is 'Do you wake the other one up to feed them when one wakes up naturally to feed, in order to keep them in synch?' Now, we started off with this mentality but eventually moved towards a baby-led approach whereby we reacted to what they wanted. Although this potentially meant that our sleep was slightly more interrupted, it seemed to mean happier babies who found their own rhythms.

For yourself, I also have some sensible advice. Realistically, your days of staying up late watching films, going out to the pub, or whatever, are at least on hold. Find your own routine to fit in harmony with your babies and don't be afraid to get early nights. It's OK, you can still be macho if you end up in bed by 9:30pm. No one needs to know! Keeping healthy and cutting down on drinking are also sound pieces of advice. You simply cannot be a good and responsible father if you are drinking every night. Here endeth the lesson.

Furthermore, don't be afraid to catch the odd cat-nap here and there. Falling asleep in front of the TV for fifteen minutes can be a vital period of recuperation.

You might want to help your partner have a rest by taking the twins out for a stroll or getting Granny over. This means that your partner can have a chance to have a half hour kip on the sofa. Serious Brownie points there.

So that's the subject of sleep in a nutshell, although there is more to mention in the section on feeding, since this is something that happens throughout the night.

Feeding: breast is best?

There is a long running dilemma over whether to really press for breastfeeding or whether to go for formula feeding with bottle. I am a massive advocate for breastfeeding and I'll tell you why.

Firstly, there are clear health benefits to breastfeeding. There are general benefits of breastfeeding, both for parent and child[1]:

- Breast milk is the only natural food designed for your baby.
- Breastfeeding protects your baby from infections and diseases.
- Breast milk provides health benefits for your baby.
- Breastfeeding provides health benefits for mum.

[1] http://www.nhs.uk/Planners/breastfeeding/Pages/why-breastfeed.aspx retrieved 09/08/2011

- It's free.
- It's available whenever and wherever your baby needs a feed.
- It's the right temperature.
- It can build a strong physical and emotional bond between mother and baby.
- It can give you a great sense of achievement.

For example, the NHS states the following health benefits for breastfeeding[1]:

- less chance of diarrhoea and vomiting and having to go to hospital as a result
- fewer chest and ear infections and having to go to hospital as a result
- less chance of being constipated
- less likelihood of becoming obese and therefore developing type 2 diabetes and other illnesses later in life
- less chance of developing eczema

There are many myths about breastfeeding that have been debunked – just see the links for the lists above for more details.

---

[1] http://www.nhs.uk/Planners/breastfeeding/Pages/health-benefits-for-baby.aspx retrieved 09/08/2011

So we can see why breastfeeding might be good for mother and twins, but what are the benefits for you, the father (other than your own children being potentially healthier)? The biggest benefit, and I cannot emphasise this enough, is that you do not have to feed the twins at night. If you were bottle-feeding your twins, you would probably be sharing the feeding duties throughout the night. However, if your twins are breastfeeding exclusively from your partner then, as a man, there is not a lot you can do to feed your twins (short of a sex change and a lot of hormone replacement drugs). This means that, especially as a working man, you may well have a much less interrupted sleep pattern and a much smoother working day. This is a massive benefit.

Now, that's not to say that you roll over and ignore all the feeds with an air of utter self-interest (er, no I didn't do that, honest...). As a man, you can offer verbal support, get the twins out of the cot and take them to your partner, or get her a drink. Helen started to breastfeed them both at the same time. As I mentioned, we woke the other twin up if the first woke up for a feed, and she fed them simultaneously. Initially, we bought a special twin breastfeeding cushion off the internet to give the proper support to Helen and the boys. However, eventually, cushions sufficed and the special pillow was made redundant. As mentioned earlier, at about three months or so, we stopped waking the second twin up to do a simultaneous feed. We did this so that they would find their own sleep rhythm and in the hope that the second twin might continue sleeping through the night. Wishful thinking since this basically didn't happen for six more months at least. Importantly, Helen also did this because they were starting to get too big to manage on her own in a drowsy state. She didn't want to drop one inadvertently onto the floor.

However, the downside to this was quite big. It meant that Helen was up very often in the night feeding the twins separately and this was a job that only she could do, and couldn't be shared with the father. Although she was occasionally expressing for those times when she wasn't around, it was slow work since her breasts were already feeding two hungry little boys. Thus the night-time feedings really were her jurisdiction. And, as I have said, this paid dividends for my own sleep.

As such, I wholeheartedly endorse breastfeeding for as long as possible, particularly the night-time feed. I now understand why one of my mates coarsely advised, with a wink, for me to "Keep them on the tit as long as possible". I now know where he was coming from. Of course, there is a time when it all looks a bit weird when children are still breastfeeding. We've all seen a documentary when five year-olds are still breastfeeding. There's definitely something a little iffy there...

There are also other massive advantages to breastfeeding. First of all, the costs. With bottle feeding, you will be paying for all the equipment and replacements, but primarily the milk. I have seen various quotes for feeding singletons ranging from £900 to £1200 a year. This will range depending on equipment, milk choice and whether you will need things like Infacol to calm tummies. Now double that, and account for gas / electricity and you can see the savings quite clearly.

Secondly, whilst breastfeeding is not only financially free (though your partner will have to eat a little more to compensate), it will also free up huge amounts of time. Washing, mixing and filling twenty bottles per day is no small task. Laborious and time consuming. This time could be used sleeping! You have been warned.

So my guide to breastfeeding concludes that it is highly beneficial to the dad. Oh, and to the twins, too.

If you do formula feed, don't feel stigmatised by uppity breastfeeding parents. There is no shame in it; it is just a bit more hassle, in my opinion. I know some mothers get a hard time and made to feel guilty over their choice. Don't let these people get to her! I cannot offer too much advice other than to keep a feeding chart of who has had what, possibly mark one bottle by putting a rubber band around it. This will allow you to know one bottle from the other with your eyes half-closed and brain half-asleep. You'll soon learn how to manipulate the twins into positions whereby you can feed them both at the same time. You'll love that bonding time, but you will also have many an interrupted night!

Nappies and poo

Nappies are no problem at all. Modern disposable nappies are compact and very easy to put on (your babies). There really isn't much to say, other than everyone has their favourites (we get eco ones if we can). You should empty the poo down the toilet before wrapping them up as well as possible so the smell does not get around and the landfill sites have less poo in them, and then put them in a perfumed nappy sack. You'll want to get changing mats and all the paraphernalia. In the end, though, you'll probably end up just changing them on the floor just as often as you use a changing mat. As long as you have a good grip on those ankles with one hand so you can wipe with the other, and get used to doing things one-handed, you'll be fine.

Remember, with girls, you must wipe front to back so you keep poo away from their bits and prevent infection.

And then there is the poo. Poo will become a major part of your life. You will stare at and analyse a lot of poo in the coming years. Your twins will start of by pooing a sticky, dark green, toffee-like substance called meconium (made up of mucus, amniotic fluid and other lovely substances and brought on by the early milk in breastfeeding, called colostrum). In many respects, even though it looks thoroughly weird, this poo is easier to clean up.

As Helen was breastfeeding, our boys used up all the milk they got to build big strong bones. Now, it is not unusual for breastfed babies to go for three or four days without pooing. However, our boys were going seven or eight days without pooing. Once, one went over three weeks without pooing. We had cleared it with a health visitor, and this does happen. When it came to the offender finally going, my, did he go...

This was actually far from being an issue. It was a godsend since we hardly ever had to change a newborn nappy – fantastic.

With bottle-fed babies, things should be more consistent, though constipation can be an issue – have a word to your health visitor if this is the case.

Newborn poo will eventually change to a lighter green colour and then to a sickly yellowish-orange colour. Eventually, when on solids, they will turn 'normal' colours.

Anything out of the normal, then consult the internet (the Baby Centre website has a very good set of poo pages, with a visual guide too![1]) and, more importantly, your health visitor or doctor (especially if there is blood).

Your twins crying

Babies cry. They always have and they always will. Crying might well be one of the hardest things to cope with for you. When you have had little sleep for a month and you're finding things difficult, and you have two screaming babies that don't seem to want to stop for love nor food, then you'll find your blood pressure rising and panic setting in. This might have something to do with everyone being a control freak to some extent. As such, you might feel a lack of control over the situation since there can sometimes be the feeling of being able to

---

[1] http://www.babycentre.co.uk/photo_galleries/baby-poo/ retrieved 09/08/2011

do nothing to solve the crying crisis. There is no verbal reasoning with two one month-olds. But there might be some things you can do. It would be a good idea to look at why babies usually cry. Normally, there are four reasons:

- Give me food! I'm hungry! You see, newborn babies have no frame of reference. They don't know what hungry is. All they have are new sensations. They don't understand what such sensations mean. In evolutionary terms, your young body not receiving food is a dangerous pastime. Thus, these poor babies will be getting hunger pains to signal that they need food. So give them food.

- I'm so tired that I'm going to shout about it and let everyone know! You'll know the feeling well, and you're going to be close to tears yourself!

- I'm too hot, too cold and I might just have pooed myself! Help! Your babies will not like being too hot or too cold, and they won't like hanging around with a crappy nappy. Be alert.

- I'm bored! Really bored! This becomes particularly prevalent the older they get. At ten months and on, our boys would cry if they didn't have toys handy, were stuck in their highchairs without anybody giving them attention and so on. Hey, it's nice to be needed, and they need you to entertain them! Dust off your one-man-band outfit and put a smile on their faces.

Other reasons to cry might include being ill or in pain, and being scared. When we first started vacuuming around the boys, Oscar was scared stiff and cried at the big, noisy monster (the vacuum, not me). Now, they both love it, and play with it as soon as it comes out. I worry when they start trying to eat it.

Illness might include things like teething. Teething can affect babies in different ways: a lot of drooling, red cheeks, diarrhoea, and some deal of crying. Tummy pains and other common illnesses might also induce a few tears. You will, however, know when your child is in *real* pain. That is a sound which pricks up the ears and gets you moving double time.

So, what to do when the crying seems to be eternal and the most brain-piercing noise you have ever heard. Now, as much as you may feel like it, never shout at your baby or get angry as this just makes it ten times worse. At the end of the day, they are trying to communicate something but just don't have the words. And never shake your baby. Ever.

So, things you can do. It does depend on the context of the crying: whether the babies are trying to sleep, whether they are playing, or simply sitting in the high chair ready to eat. One of the most useful techniques is the distraction technique. "Ooh, look at this toy car, Oscar! Wow, how amazing it is! Vroom Vroom!" often does the trick. Take their minds off whatever it is that is getting their goat. This is also a great tactic to use in the classroom whenever a naughty child is about to do something bad, as any teacher will tell you.

Putting music on, the vacuum or some other continuous noise might also help. If it doesn't stop them crying, it might just help to drown out the incessant noise!

Many parents rely on taking their baby out for a drive or for a walk in the buggy. This is not so easy with twins. You will find out, for sure, that putting twins in the buggy or car takes twice as long than for singletons. However, if your partner is at hand, and you only have one crier, then this could be a good option. The rocking movement of the car and buggy simulates the rocking that they would have experienced in your partner's womb and this will lull them to sleep, dreaming of a warm and cosy place.

Of course, if it's sleep time, then rocking, singing lullabies and talking gently to the baby might help. This was rather like throwing a cup of water at a towering inferno in the case of our Oscar, but a useful tool for some people, nonetheless.

There is a national charity called Cry-sis (http://www.cry-sis.org.uk/) which has phone lines open every day to deal with distraught parents of even more distraught babies.

At the end of the day, they're probably crying because they are hungry or tired. Not too dissimilar to us, really.

The talk of the town

Twins are special and doesn't everybody know it. You'd better get used to being special, the talk of the town. Well, not strictly speaking *you*, but you're delightful duo. This is wonderful, as it gives you a chance to show off the fruit of your loins to anyone who cares. Which is a surprising amount of people. This can come both as a delight, but also with its caveats.

Firstly, when you get out about town, if you decide to go to the shopping centre for a few bits and pieces (and a welcome break from the house) then be sure to add an extra 45 minutes or so onto your shopping time. Especially when the twins are younger, and if they are wearing the same clothes, people will stop you *all of the time*. It is quite amazing to behold but total strangers will have no issue stopping you in the street or in the shopping centre to make a fuss over your babies. Don't take your twins out if you are in a hurry to do the shopping. In fact, don't take your twins out if you are in a hurry to do anything!

You'll notice that most people, if they don't stop you, will at least smile sweetly at your cherubs. Twins have a miraculous capability to enthral everyone. Strangely, when using the double pram, we had as many people stopping us to check out our pram as to check out the babies!

You'll find that people will start knowing or recognising you, especially if you live in a smaller place. People who you don't really know will be asking after your twins. As one internet poster said, "Babies are indeed chick magnets. But the chicks are mostly under 16 or over 60."

You can broadly fit people into two categories: those who say, "Oh, I wish I'd had twins" and those who say, “Jesus, mate, I don’t know how you do it – I can’t cope with one!”

People will talk to you and your partner about twins, or babies in general. They will, no doubt, offer all sorts of advice. Some of this will be fine, but much of it is often stupid, annoying or patently ridiculous. This is because people who have not had twins (or even children) giving advice to parents of twins is a pointless exercise. Chalk and cheese.

Common comments (that might irritate you)

1. It’s easy, it’s just like having two single babies.

2. Are they twins? (No, one is made out of cardboard. We just carry him around as company for the other one. The other great thing to say, if you have the guts, is no, they both have separate fathers. Ha! Or tell them they are triplets, but you sold one...)

3. Are they identical? (No-one can tell your twins apart like you, evidently. This is even funnier if you have boy / girl twins. Yes, it does happen. Just say, no, one has a penis.)

4. Were they conceived naturally, or with fertility medication? (Er, what position did you conceive your child in, since we’re obviously close enough to be personal? Even worse, some have been

known to ask "Are they real?" as in naturally conceived! Sheesh.)

5. I have two children close in age so I know JUST what it's like to have twins! (No you don't.)

6. Which one is your favourite / smarter / more annoying? (Alright when they are young, but no-one likes being compared to their siblings.)

7. Having twins is easy, they entertain themselves.

8. I've got two dogs, it must be the same as having twins. (Seriously, a woman said that to a mother at twins club down at the park.)

However, having said this, there are a lot of forums and websites with parents (mothers) of twins spouting off about questions that annoy the hell out of them. I think that most of these parents are just too miserable or touchy and need to get over themselves. Enjoy the questions, especially if they are stupid. Come up with comedy answers each time. Enjoy the spotlight, because the older they get, the less people will care. Babies are cute, toddlers less so, 5 year-olds should be seen and not heard (at least, so many people think).

Changes to your life

Your life will change, as I am sure you have worked out. There is no denying it, and it would be unfair on your twins to insist that it did not. This includes work, rest and play.

Firstly, you are now a family (if these are your first). If they are your first, your family size has just doubled. Nice one. However, you may not now be the number one priority in the eyes of your partner. There are two little ones who have jumped the queue to being the apples of her eyes. Not only that, but you need to continue to put her first, as I am sure you were doing over the pregnancy. Although you have your two new little ones, your partner will need some looking after to aid her recovery.

I was a keen rugby player, amongst many other things, and this was one of the things that had to go. I may have put on a bit of weight as a result, but it allowed me to devote more time to the new family. This is not permanent, but certainly for at least the first year, my visits to the rugby club were seldom and for social purposes only. These are the sorts of compromises that will be essential. It may be a sport, hobby, work commitments or whatever, but twins involve a good deal of give and take.

Actually, work is an important sphere of life to balance. It is really important that work understand the difficulties of bringing up twins. The lack of sleep, the demands of time – you will need to be supported by work. It may be that a flexible working arrangement might be handy. If you work shifts then this could be used to your advantage in some way.

One of the oft mentioned pieces of advice, particularly from other men, is that there will be a severe drought on the sex front. Tiredness from interrupted nights, the demands of two babies, fatigue from breastfeeding and looking after children all day; all of this contributes to an environment not conducive to sex. This will be even more evident if she has had a C-section as she will need extra time to recover. Firstly, if this is the case then don't feel that all physicality must stop. Hugs and kisses go a long way to support a tired mum. Secondly, it doesn't have to be so – it's just a case of picking your time or making time.

Essentially, as tough as twins can be, you don't want them to come between you, and juggling everybody's needs, including yours, is an important task for the two of you.

"Is there anything we can do to help?"

Er, yes. These are wonderful words to hear. Do not, I repeat, do not be too proud to accept help from family or friends. "No, it's fine, we're OK" is just silly and you'll regret it. My sister has emigrated to New Zealand and she is presently expecting twins. Although NZ is an amazing place, she will be at a distinct disadvantage as to have only half the family to draw support from. She also lives about an hour north of Auckland in the sticks, so she will find it even harder. Luckily, her mother-in-law has agreed to live with them for three days a week to help out, which is awesome.

In our case, both sets of parents are alive and well and living in close proximity. As such, they are a tremendous help. Helen's parents (Ivan and Margaret) are in the lucky position of now being retired. However, they are busier now than they probably ever have been due to the time spent supporting us. I cannot tell you how lucky we are to have our housework done on a daily basis, and the garden looking fantastic, brimming with lovely fruit and vegetables. In fact, our home and garden are looking better now than before Helen was pregnant. To make matters better, Helen has two older children from a previous relationship who, with their partners, provide excellent support when around with babysitting to give us a break, or simply just to help us out.

Without such support, I would never have written this book. It means that Helen can concentrate on making really tasty and healthy food for the boys, seeing to their every need and mothering them in the best way that she can. I can go to work and get back to a clean house and two happy boys, and a less stressed and happier partner. Win / win.

Of course, the other benefit of extended help is that the children get used to being handled by other people and their social skills improve. Statistically, it has been shown that twins receive less individual attention than singletons. This can possibly have ramifications on their speech development and other abilities. As a result, the added individual attention they get from having extra helpers around is hugely beneficial.

Here are some ways in which people can help you get through the week:

- Meals. Either prepared and brought around, or prepared in your own kitchen whilst the two of you get on and do twin things.
- Housework and gardening. Oh yes, if they are willing, will them.

- Donations of clothing, equipment and toys. People have some wonderful stuff hanging around, waiting to be given away. We were given two whole bin liners full of various and electronic toys.
- Visits. Babysitting of sorts, but you stay in the house to do other things or nap.
- Babysitting. Same as above, but you leave the house with your partner and enjoy some *you* time. Watch a film, have a meal. Go on, enjoy yourself.
- Buying stuff is always nice, whether it be nappies here or there, baby clothes, or whatever. All gifts kindly received.
- General support. Help with feeding (er, not breast), talking, walking, playing, making sure they know their Russian alphabet by 6 months etc.
- Running errands.
- Help with visitors. This was important during the first few months. We had LOADS of visitors and we also had family to help make tea and cut the cake for all the people hungry to cuddle the twins.

I suppose the big challenge is whether you still receive the help after the twins lose their 'hey, they've got twins!' charm.

It is such a valuable thing to be sharing the delights of your twins with others, too, and it can help bring extended families together which is no bad thing.

Twindividuality

One of the most common issues and subjects for discussion with regards to twins is how to dress them and how to give them a sense of individuality, especially if they are identical. And people will differ on their opinions here. I, for one, get a shiver of unease down my spine when I see adult twins wearing the same clothes. Really? Honestly? Sheesh, get a life.

Yet it's a different kettle of fish when they are babies. I started off with the mentality that they would never wear the same clothes and that they would have a clear sense of individuality supported by their variety in clothing. However, at that age, they don't really know their cardigans from their nappies and I actually compromised to some degree on the clothing front. It's also difficult when so many people give you pairs of the identical clothes as presents. This is obviously not the case with boy / girl twins!

There is also a marked difference to other people's attitudes when they see the babies in the pram with identical knitted cardigans and hats. Identical clothing is a marker that tells people 'these children are twins' and they can react with confidence and joy.

Often, the twins might be wearing the same tops but different trousers, or we use pairs of clothes to dress the same twin in but allow for a change out of dirty, dribbled-on clothing throughout the day. Another idea is to buy similar outfits that are not identical; for example, the same pattern but in two different colours or simply similar styles of clothes. It can also be a good idea, when they are a bit older, to share their clothes to promote the idea of sharing. And of course, from time to time, it is nice to dress them identically, admittedly. Let them choose their clothes if possible.

As for the broader picture of twindividuality, well, what is it? Your twins will spend most of their formative lives together – feeding, sleeping, playing, travelling, in the buggy, bathing and so on. It would be too unmanageable not to be so. However, as they grow older, parents often feel the pressure to instil a sense of individuality in their twins. Although some experts say that the twins will eventually do this for themselves, there are some strategies to help ensure that your twins aren't clones devoid of their own, personal differences.

Some parents prefer their twins not to be seen as a set, or 'the twins', but as two distinct individuals, and these tips can help you achieve that goal. This will be all the more important if your twins are identical, as they are more likely to have similar looks (obviously!) and personalities. There can be practical applications of twindividuality. If you see one twin running towards the road and you cannot identify at a glance which one, then you cannot quickly warn them by shouting their name. It may seem ridiculous, but a little thing like that can have great consequences.

You can also teach your twins to say their names as early as possible if they are identical or similar. In that way, they can correct people who get their names wrong themselves. Getting your children used to spending short time periods apart can also be a useful tip so they don't have a total dependency on each other.

Top Tips to promote twindividuality

1. Clothes. Avoid dressing them identically, especially as they get older. This may be in clothing as a whole, or with shoes, jumpers bibs etc. The key word might be 'similar' rather than 'identical'.

2. Hair styles. This is where you can give your twins choices. Allow them to define how they want their hair. This can be an important defining mark of individuality for them.

3. Avoid giving them labels such as "the twins" or "the boys / girls" by using their individual names as often as possible. Some suggest not giving them identifiable characteristic labels such as "This one's the sporty one".

4. Praise each twin individually. Don't tar one twin with the brush of the other twin. Ensure that the praise is fairly given to each and obvious. This might also promote the

other to carry out the desired behaviour when they witness the praise given to their sibling. This applies to punishments too...

5. Give good one-on-one attention to each twin. Don't give one all the love whilst locking the other in a cupboard. No one likes that. This might mean the odd trip down the park with one whilst the other does something individual with your partner or other member of the family. It is also wise to get two individual strollers when they are a bit older.

6. Promote a nurturing of their own specific interests. If they have different interests or preferences, don't ignore this in the hunt for an easy life. This is an important area to look at supporting their individual needs.

7. Birthdays. These double celebrations must not be seen as a single unit occasion. Have two cakes, two sets of presents and cards and two bad renditions of Happy Birthday. This stretches to other children's birthdays. Make sure that you get two presents and

cards, one from each of your twins. It doesn't have to be expensive – cheaper presents or ones that come in two parts are great.

8. Encourage them to have separate friendships if the opportunity arises. When they are older, you can do this concurrently. One invites friends around whilst the other goes to a friend's house.

9. As any teacher would do and say, adjust your expectations for each based on what they are like. Don't judge one by the standards of the other. It is especially important not to compare one to the other so as to foster resentment between them – "Archie's much better at croquet than you, Tarquin."

10. This is a nice one to do – preserve individual memories. We have two separate photo albums that we have taken individual photos of them doing normal things – brushing their teeth, sleeping, playing. This shows their development on an individual

basis.

11. Identify possessions. When they are a little older, make sure they are aware of which things belong to whom, such as toys and books. Introducing rules on property and privacy will help underscore sharing and looking after and being responsible for their own belongings.

12. Nurture their twin-ness too! Single-mindedly trying to turn them into complete individuals may do more harm than good, so don't forget they are twins, and that they will have a special bond.

Gadgets and gizmos

No advice to blokes would be complete without a foray into the world of 'technology'. Well, by technology, I mean battery operated kids' toys or breastpumps. Obviously, many of these gizmos, such as the aforementioned breastpump, aren't so relevant to dads. I suppose the useful gadgets are those which make our lives easier, or keep the children quiet.

As the years have advanced in the world of baby shops and baby products, there have been growing numbers of amazing and wonderful gadgets marketed at new parents. Now it's got to the stage where there is something for every occasion. There is little chance of saying "I wish they'd invent something that could do that!" because, trust me, they already have.

I'll list a few items and their descriptions giving some reasons why they are good additions to the twin household.

- Firstly, the most useful thing has been the internet. If we ever wanted to know anything about babies or twins, and knowing how to use the internet well, we were able to find answers to anything. So very valuable.

- The electronic activity centre (we have a Leap Frog one) has been a real bonus. We bought one off ebay as they can cost a few bob. This is a circular activity centre with a material bucket-type seat in the centre. The child in the middle can rotate around to different 'toys' which make various sounds and do various things. This is such a good toy because it occupies one child for a fairly long period whilst you can concentrate on doing something with the other twin, or something else entirely. It is also really useful for sensory development and hand-eye coordination. Thumbs up.

- Aqua-Pod Duo. This is a suckered mat with two seats with suckers on themselves which stick up through the mat. This is essential bath equipment for parents of twins because it allows just one of you to bath both twins if needs be. Even with both of you there, bathing is so much easier as the children can sit up unaided whilst being able to play with bath toys. Splish splash, spend that cash.

- Playpen. We bought a playpen off a work colleague and, although our twins don't like being left alone in it locked up for too long (they crave our attention), it is very useful if you need to do something important, you're on your own, and you need to keep the twins safe and entertained. With a comfy mat (which comes with it) and plenty of toys, it can be a playtastic item.

- A decent handheld vacuum cleaner. A good powerful Dustbuster or similar is an essential tool for any twin or baby parent. Meal times are particularly messy and require much cleaning.

- A baby walker. We have a Vtech electronic baby walker. This is a four-wheeled machine that looks like a stroller that the babies can push whilst cruising (standing up, but needing to hold on to something). This encourages them to learn the rudiments of walking without continually faceplanting on the floor. Moreover, it has a front face which can be detached that has lots of buttons, gadgets and switches that can be pressed for a vivid array of sounds and effects.

- Stair gates and more stair gates. Put 'em up everywhere. Not only does it give you a chance to get out your drill and feel like a man, but it stops your twins falling down stairs, climbing up stairs, entering the kitchen when you are busy cooking a storm or walking out the back door and impaling themselves on a stray rake.

- Cupboard locks. Cheap and useful for cupboards with all the chemicals in. Typically, this is the only cupboard they really want to go in. They have a sixth sense for most wanting to do the thing which they are most prohibited from doing!

- This is the genius of Helen's father. I went out one day to come back and find all the doors had a curved protective barrier on them to stop the boys denting their heads on the corners. This was so simple and so effective because the boys have head-butted these protective covers ample times to no avail. All that he made them from was white plastic piping sliced down and parted to stretch over the door edge. Genius and as cheap as chips whilst looking like a professional product.

- Reins can be a particularly useful tool, especially when out with you children about town as the only adult. It means you can keep them close enough to control and keep them safe. Some people feel they are like walking a pair of dogs, but they have certainly got their use.

So these were and are some of the things that we certainly found useful with the arrival of our boys.

Always remember to stay one step ahead of the development of your twins when childproofing your house. Take those keys out of the locks before they can reach and turn them. Don't be reactive, be proactive!

From left to right, baby walker, playpen and activity centre.

Twin Club

Virtually every area in Britain has some form of twin club and it is worth giving them a special mention. Twin clubs are voluntary groups of parents of twins, usually mostly mothers, who have weekly gatherings. They provide support networks and arrange all manner of things, depending on the group.

In our local group, for example, there is a weekly morning alternating between two local venues (a Sure Start centre and a Nursery) where parents bring their twins. The mornings are equipped with lots of toys, activities (arts and crafts for the older ones) and things to do. However, the main reasons for going aren't just to entertain the children (though this is a brilliant way of getting them out of the house and interacting with other children), but to give you or you partner a break and an excuse to get out of the house. Even more important is the opportunity to meet other parents of twins who are further along the journey than you and from whom you can garner really useful advice.

Being a parent of twins has many challenges and it is unchartered territory for most parents. As such, there is so much the average parent doesn't know and so very many questions to ask that twin club really is a vital ingredient to successfully navigate having twins.

Another obvious benefit to twin clubs is the opportunity to get hold of or get rid of useful twin and baby equipment. There will come a time when you will need to get hold of something you desperately need or sell on something that your twins have grown out of. Twin clubs can be like a hassle-free eBay amongst friends. It's great to find out what works, as far as equipment is concerned, and what is not worth the effort or money. This goes for simple advice about anything – there is a wealth of it at twin club. No one knows or understands the life of a parent of twins better than... a parent of twins.

There are usually parties and get-togethers at Easter, Halloween and Christmas and so on. Summer barbecues are fun and a good excuse to get out with the twins in a safe and comfortable environment. You need to teach the children from an early age that it is the stereotypically male job to burn the sausages whilst talking nonsense to whoever cares to listen.

At our twin club, we are also sorting out discounts with local businesses for the members of the club. Having twins is expensive – two of everything at the same time. As a result, it is great when companies realise this and offer a second child half price or similar. If it wasn't for twin club, we would not have known that a local swimming school set-up offers the second twin half price for swimming lessons in a private hydro-therapy heated pool, where the instructor only has a maximum of four children. Result!

This and many other discounts have been or are being organised by our twin club.

Ben's Top Five Tips

Ben Marsh is a dad from the Gosport and Fareham Twin Club, my local twin club. He has devised a list of tips to offer any prospective dad of twins:

1. **Recognise when your partner needs help -** Whether they are babies or small children: there are days when you will have had the day from hell at work and you come home to find your partner almost in tears or tearing their hair out because of the twins. This is when you can be a knight in shining armour and give them a break, let them have some time out to calm down and relax. Put your bad day on the back burner and when the kids are in bed then you can both have a moan about your respective days.

2. **Do not suffer in silence -** Drop the

big-man macho act - it fools no-one, especially other parents when they can see you're having problems. Twins are harder work than a single child, so don't be afraid to ask for help from parents, family, friends or even neighbours. For example, Hermione (one of our twin daughters) was running a very high fever during the snow and neither of our cars could make it in the snow the two miles to the doctors. Fortunately, one of our neighbours had a 4x4 and was only too happy to take Max (my wife) and Hermione up to the doctor's.

3. **Don't have a favourite** - It seems obvious advice but is easier said than done: the worst thing you can do is have a favourite, they are both your little miracles. Don't always bath one of your children. Take it in turns with each child. Don't always put the same one to bed - this can lead to problems in the future if you are left to put the babies / children to bed on your own and Child A will only have cuddles with mummy. If the children choose their favourite then that's their choice but you still need to divide your love equally.

4. **Routine, Routine, Routine** - I know every book you will read or have read says this, but it is essential with twins. Get the routine established

early they will learn it very quickly and it is amazing how much easier it is to get them down to sleep in the evening. Get your pattern and times sorted and you can start to get your evenings back sooner, rather than later.

5. **Local Twin Club -** A top must. Your health visitor can give you general advice, your parents and friends will all give loads of advice; but unless they have twins, they have no idea what you are going through. Your local Twin Club can be your best place for support and advice because every parent there is a parent of twins. Some will have children of the same age, some slightly older and some a year or two older - there is a wealth of knowledge within these clubs. No-one will claim to be an expert but they know what you are going through and will always be happy to support and help where they can.

TAMBA

The Twins and Multiple Births Association (TAMBA) is a charity group well-worth joining. They provide excellent support and information to parents of twins or multiples. For example, we joined and were able to download some excellent pdf booklets on pregnancy, birth, breastfeeding and so on, all produced for parents of twins, and jam-packed full of useful information. The advice on offer ranges from pregnancy right through to primary school ages for twins.

TAMBA also run courses in selected parts of the country which may be of use.

As well as being a fount of knowledge, TAMBA also offer their members good discounts with their membership card, such as at Clark's. Twins make shopping for things like shoes very expensive indeed, so any help is gratefully received!

Ben's best and worst buys

When they are little:

1. Upgrade your car - Max started off with a Fiesta, but now owns a Galaxy. It's easier to get the shopping, buggy, girls and the dog into one car, but it's also a good investment because it's a car you will need for a long time. And, when it's raining, she can get in the dry and put them into their seats rather than getting soaked outside.

2. Nipper 360 Double Buggy - now this

really is a marmite buggy, you either love it or hate it. But for us it was a top buy because (a) we do a lot of off-road walking and (b) at 9kg its one of the lightest buggies on the market and as Max is quite small it meant she could lift it easily - weight is a factor for any double buggy.

3. A glider chair. It's nice and comfy for those late night feeds and when you are with them for hours during the night.

4. Nappy Genie (a nappy disposal system) - picture the scene: its mid-December, blowing a gale outside, throwing it down & you've just changed your fourth stinky nappy in an hour. Do you really want to have to go outside to your bin or go to a sealed bin, that doesn't smell in the nursery or better yet the bathroom or toilet? - nuff said.

5. Tumble dryer - trying to get everything dry in the middle of winter is not easy especially now your washing load has tripled.

As they get older:

6. Cot Beds - A big investment given that you need two, but they will last them until they are 5ish.

7. Port-a-potty - potty training two little children is bad enough, but if you get caught out in the middle of town, country or theme park and you can't

find a toilet or have to wait to use one, then accidents will happen, but a port-a-potty saves you that worry. It also helps when you know that you can't get two of them to walk fast enough to get to the toilets in time.

8. High Chair ties - a portable fold away in a small bag high chair that ties onto a normal chair. It's bad enough having to fight other parents for one high chair that might be available at the café, but with these you just need two normal chairs.

9. Dan Dan Chairs - we bought these too late. We wasted money on booster seats on normal chairs but Dan Dan chairs are definitely the way forward and again will last them for years. A friend of ours eldest used hers until she was eight.

10. Body reins - when they are learning to walk and lose their balance so often it's easier to save them on body reins rather on wrist reins, which could hurt them. Not only that, it was far easier to pick them up bodily and put them down in the same place and facing the same direction! A godsend with two who wanted to walk at different speeds in different directions.

And a few things not to buy:

11. Any pregnancy book that wasn't aimed specifically at twins. You only get two pages of twin stuff if you're lucky and most of the other stuff isn't

relevant! Better to invest in a twin specific book at the start, or better still, borrow them!

12. Pricy travel cots. We bought one that was all singing and dancing for when we brought them home to have in our room, but maybe used it about six times? We then needed a second one because they were too big to share and we were going on holiday and that one was a much cheaper one - still did the same job! Only real difference was the more expensive one had a bassinette feature, which we could only use at the beginning anyway before they tried to climb out!

13. Cot mobiles - only last for twenty minutes and we could never get the music to coincide. Nightmare. We have a bubble fish tube with floating fish and changing lights and classical music CDs. The music was far more portable when travelling away from home as well.

Feeding

Feeding time at the zoo can be a stressful and very messy time indeed. Feeding one child is testing, feeding two is tough. Obviously, there is a difference between feeding your babies when they are newborn and feeding them as toddlers. If your partner is breastfeeding, then the important thing is to make sure your partner is eating really well; that means a balanced and healthy diet. This is exceptionally vital during pregnancy as your babies' organs are being created in the womb and require decent building blocks to do their jobs properly. However, it is still a really essential thing for your partner to do whilst breastfeeding. I have talked a little about how this can positively impact your babies' health. The human body (well, the female body) is pretty efficient at producing milk, so your partner will need to up her calories, but not by a huge amount. It also depends from person to person. It's worth talking to your health visitor to get the latest advice.

The older they get, though, the more logistical it becomes. We tried to make sure they ate as healthily as possible, which meant cooking things freshly with good ingredients. In fact, the boys eat better than us. However, this does mean that my partner spends much time cooking. Obviously, it is advisable, if cooking for your twins rather than relying on jars and suchlike, to cook more than necessary and freeze in portion-sized plastic containers. Investment in all sizes (or eating a lot of Chinese meals and keeping the boxes) is a good idea. Sometimes, a whole Sunday morning or afternoon is spent cooking for the week ahead. It helps to be organised.

It also helps to get some really good non-drip cups. If your twins are anything like our boys, then cups get banged and shaken, and if they have any kind of free-flow cups then you will have juice all over the walls and carpet.

Furthermore, feeding time is messy. We have taken to putting a groundsheet (a small piece of tarpaulin that their Granddad bought) underneath the two high chairs which sit side by side. This means that the carpet does not get ruined as the tarp can be wiped clean or shaken out.

We started by feeding both babies from the same bowl for ease of practice so that one of us can be clearing up as well. However, it is also nice to be able to feed them together from separate bowls. As they get older, it is important to let them investigate their food. I remember seeing a documentary on parenting (one of those things you do to appease your other half, though it soon becomes apparent that you find them just as fascinating). On the show, there was a couple who were struggling to get their child to eat healthy food. The child would have a tantrum as he sat there, being made to eat the healthy food almost as an adult, not being allowed to make a big mess. As the child kicked up such a fuss, the parents gave in and allowed the toddler to sit on the sofa and munch on junk. A food psychologist then invited the parents to a session. At this session, they were invited to taste some unknown foods shown to them in ramekins. These foods were presented in such a way as not to be recognisable. What did the adults do? They prodded and pushed the foods, feeling their textures and investigating them BEFORE putting them in their mouths. And yet they were not allowing their child to do this with its healthy food. As a result of the session, the parents went away with the idea that it was good to let their child play with and investigate their food as a way of understanding it and being able to better appreciate it. The parents also took an active role in investigating different foodstuffs with the child. The end result was that the child started eating good, healthy food, albeit a little more messily.

This investigation is also vital to train your twins in self-feeding. We ended up often giving the boys a little bit of food in their own bowls with their own spoons whilst we fed them the majority of the food from bowls which we were holding. A good self-feeding training opportunity.

A good food processor and blender are prerequisites for baby feeding, and some good baby cook books, such as Annabel Karmel's books (or similar). We started steaming vegetables for the boys to eat early on, and now they just love to chomp on steamed carrots, broccoli or beans. What a joy it is to see a toddler enjoy something so healthy! Long may it continue. Personally, much of the problem with our young eating so poorly these days is the result of the parents not eating well. To justify their own poor diet, they impress it upon their children which, in turn, brings out a sort of co-dependence.

It is also wise, if you are watching your own weight, to be mindful of finishing off your own babies' leftovers. Doing this everyday is a sure way to sneak in those extra inches. Tasty, though.

Going out

Whether it be going out for a quick half an hour to the local park or a day trip to the seaside, there is some useful advice to the would-be 'I can do anything' dad that I know you are.

Going out with your partner and the twins is fine. She organises the changing bag. Nice. And the food. Great. And the spare clothes. Awesome. And the toys, too. Wahey! At least you've filled the car with petrol, so you're not *that* useless. However, going out solo, sans missus is a whole different ball game. Something worth remembering is that children don't really need a massive day out to feel like they have been out. In fact, they'd barely recognise the difference between the local park and a day trip to Alton Towers. Don't overdo it unnecessarily.

If there are two of you, it might be easier to have two single strollers rather than one big double buggy. This is certainly the case for shopping trips where negotiating people and racks of clothes is an art-form.

You see, looking after the twins in the safe confines of your own home is one thing, but venturing out into the big, wide and, frankly, rather dangerous world is entirely another. I remember taking the twins out on a windy autumnal Thursday afternoon to the local play park. I knew there would be no one there as it was a mid-afternoon school day. I was right, as empty as the average reality TV star's head. Getting them there was fine. The checklist is pretty simple for those basic hours out:

Changing bag complete with:

- Nappies
- Nappy sacks
- Baby powder to make their bums smell nice after changing them
- Fold-up changing mat

And then:

- Toys attached to the buggy (that they summarily ignore)
- Jumpers
- Shoes and socks
- Drinks
- Snacks

And that's it, really. Not too difficult. I mean, the first time I went out, I forgot the drinks and snacks. You don't forget them a second time; especially if you let slip your misdemeanour to your other half.

So you're off whistling down the road, over the traffic lights, down the other road, and onto the grass and into the park. Gate shut, jobs a goodun'. And then you realise that you are in charge of two toddlers on your own in a park. It's a small park: swings, baby swings, slide, see-saw, soft tarmac, chain thingies, rope thingies and the usual stuff. But you simply cannot be in two places at once. You see singleton parents at parks, religiously following their child like a doting ugly shadow. Easy. But trying to follow two toddlers running off in separate directions is non too easy. It's particularly difficult when they are in that 'just learnt to walk and investigate everything' stage. This is the stage where they will simply not look at their feet when they are charging around.

All this means that you have one toddler walking blindly into a chain which is up to his knees, falling full pelt over it and face-planting onto the tarmac, whilst the other is alternating from putting his hands in the bin to sitting in a puddle. And you are dithering between the two like Buridan's Ass.

When you have to change one of their nappies, do you strap the other into the constraints of the buggy, or let him run free and enjoy himself. This means you have your hands full with the legs and pooey bum of one child, whilst the other has realised he can climb three-quarters of the way up the soaking-wet slide to teeter agonisingly dangerously on the edge.

The end result? About an hour of pure stress. In a play park, where fun is the order of the day.

The moral of the story? Get two adults if there is any way you can. Borrow someone (a partner, a granddad, a friend, a neighbour, a stranger, a homeless man drinking white lightning at the park...).

PART IV – BEYOND TODDLERS

All too quickly, those baby months are over and your twins are suddenly toddlers. All too quickly again, your toddlers are suddenly twin children, and you are no longer stopped in the street by old ladies cooing over your 'delightful bundles'.

Hopefully, your twins have their own healthy identities, and may have vastly different characteristics, or be very similar in many ways. Or a bit of both. New challenges will present themselves, and this is where we are at the moment. It is hard, therefore, to discuss much of this section from first hand experience. However, I have gathered enough information from good sources, and I know a good deal of twins' parents to be able to make this an informative section of the book. It depends on when you do certain things with your children as to whether some of this information will be relevant for this section or the previous one (for example, you might send your children to nursery as young toddlers).

Nursery

Sending your children off to nursery for the first time is always a tough day. Seeing them cry when you leave and thinking about how much they are missing you is hard. Even though they clearly won't care as they stick their hands in jelly, build bricks to knock them down, and paint prints of their hands on sugar paper.

Invariably, your children will be fine and the time away from their stressed-out parents socialising with other children will be time well-spent. The only issues with regard to twins are the normal ones – those of logistics and cost. The price of nurseries is expensive enough. This cost is near enough doubled, assuming you get a paltry 10% discount for the second child. Obviously, having twins is financially similar to having two children close in age with things like this. However, there are less clothing hand-me downs and everything happens at the same time. The government, at the time of writing, offer a scheme whereby you can pay out for your nursery costs from your wages before your tax is deducted. This means that your tax deductions will be lower thus saving some cash for you.

Logistically, dropping your twins off at the nursery can be difficult, especially on your own. This is the same for any trip out. If your nursery has security doors, it can be a struggle holding two children and all their stuff whilst trying to negotiate thumb recognition doorways!

As they get a little older, spend the time teaching them individually to dress themselves. These little bits of independence are vital for helping both them and you.

If your twins are identical or very similar, help out the staff and the other children by making sure they have distinguishing features, whether it be clothing or hairstyles. This might mean that they are identifiable from a distance in an emergency. This will apply later, too, for when they are at school. It may be easy for you to recognise the difference between your twins after three or four years of knowing them, but this is not the same for others who have rarely seen them. You might also need to take the time to explain to staff how to tell them apart. Obviously, it is wise to communicate any needs, such as delayed language, with staff as well.

Other than that, nurseries offer few challenges particular to twins and parents of twins, and a great opportunity for them to interact with other peers.

Primary School

So, big school approaches. Parents of twins usually have lots to say about primary schools and what it means to twins.

First and foremost, what can you do to prepare your children for school? Well, sadly enough, research suggests that twins lag behind in their language, reading and writing skills when compared to singletons. This can be for many reasons, such as having received less individual attention; having spent so much time with their multiple sibling and thus learning off them rather than a more knowledgeable adult; having less time to put across their point thus making their sentences shorter; one child assuming the role of speaking on behalf of the other; and of course the fact that they may have been premature, and all the ramifications which can go with that. This means that you have to work harder, with your partner or extended family, or any adults who can help, on reading and general language skills. Get learning your phonic skills with your twins, both individually and together. You can pick up any number of resources to help you here, such as flash cards, games and suchlike to make the experience all the more interactive. Number recognition, as well as letters and colours and other basic skills, are essential things to learn. Use a wide range of vocabulary with your twins as too many children are entering school these days with a paucity of vocab. Here is a table which states the expected language development of children[1]:

Age	Language development
2	Uses 50 or more recognisable words, and understands many more. Pays attention when people talk to him, and begins to listen to more general talk. Carries out simple instructions. Puts two or more words together in simple sentences. Refers to self by name. Talks continually during play, although much may be incomprehensible. Asks the names of people and objects. Knows the names of body parts, and can name familiar pictures and objects on request.
2 ½	Uses 200 recognisable words, although articulation and grammar are immature. Can give full name. Talks during play. Uses pronouns correctly. Asks "what?" and "who?" questions. Enjoys familiar stories and rhymes.
3	Has a large vocabulary which is intelligible to strangers, although sound substitutions and immature grammar are common. Can give full name, sex and age. Uses pronouns, plurals and

[1]*Twins, triplets and more Years 2,3 & 4,* TAMBA 2006

	prepositions correctly. Asks "what?", "where?" and "who?" questions. Listens eagerly to stories. Knows several nursery rhymes. Can count up to 10.
4	Speech is grammatically correct and completely intelligible. Can give an account of recent events and experiences. Can give full name, address and age. Asks "how?", "when?" and "why?" questions. Asks what words mean. Listens to and tells long stories - both fact and fantasy - and knows several nursery rhymes. Enjoys jokes. Can count up to 20.

Another way to prepare them is to help build up their attention spans. As with the above issues, twins are susceptible to attention problems. Possibly, this is because many are born prematurely. This may be responsible for much of this sort of data with twins. Moreover, being twins, they are constantly entertaining (or being distracted by) each other. You might well realise that one or both twins might have some kind of attention deficit. This is considerably more common with boys. Consult a professional if you have any worries and they can tell you what activities are appropriate for your child or children. You'd be surprised how many children can be anecdotally diagnosed by reception teachers years before any official diagnosis for special needs.

It can be the case for twins, because of the extra cost, that they do not get to experience nursery or pre-school before going to school. This can mean that they do not have an understanding of the routine or the etiquette involved in school life and the transition from home to school can be more difficult. Good nurseries can prepare your twins for sitting quietly in a circle for circle time, teach them how to raise their hands, interact with other children and so on.

And then there is the actual primary school. Even though twins and multiples are on the increase, schools (and remember, I am a primary school teacher and so have some experience in this field!) rarely have anything that approaches a policy with regards to multiples.

The main question is this: should twins be separated or kept together in school classes? It is difficult because teachers seem to be divided, themselves, as to which is the best way forward for twins. Many schools separate twins on behest of the parents, many of whom believe that the children's independence will develop beneficially, helping with problems of one twin dominating or restricting the other. On the other hand, others seek to keep them together for mutual support or even because there is no good reason to separate them.

And then many schools don't talk about it to parents at all – it's just business as usual.

It seems like it is horses for courses. This is because twin relationships can come in many different shapes and sizes, sometimes broadly categorised as:

- Closely coupled: almost like one child
- Extreme individuals: hate being twins
- Mature dependents: happy twin/single

Most people generally seem to want to develop their twins into the third category, the mature dependent – twins who are happy being twins but who can develop as individuals, making their own friends and so on.

Another point to make is to ensure that the school always provides separate times for parent's evenings as it is important to separate their needs and give them the individual time that they deserve.

Obviously, the question of separating your twins becomes irrelevant if your local school is a one-form entry school or smaller! Otherwise, though, it is worth sitting down with your reception teacher and discussing the options. You can separate them, keep them together, or start them together and separate them later.

Let me now defer to the NHS who provide this information[1]:

Keeping twins together

A recent survey conducted by Kings College London found that twins separated at the start of primary school had more emotional problems on average than twins who were kept together. This was particularly noticeable in identical twins.

Although not all twins were affected, and some may benefit from separation, it's important to take into account the personality of your children when making your decision. It's also important to discuss your children's wishes and ensure that these are taken into account when you make a decision.

The benefits of keeping twins together at school include:

- Twins often settle faster in school if they're kept together. If they like being together, there are definite advantages to keeping them in the same class.
- Twins who don't want to be separated will suffer if they're forced apart. This may make them

[1] http://www.nhs.uk/Livewell/twins-and-multiples/Pages/school-separation.aspx (retrieved 5/10/11)

more dependent on each other.

- If twins are highly dependent and would be distressed to be separated, it's better to keep them together.
- Twins tend to be competitive. If this becomes excessive, it makes sense to separate them, but a mild rivalry can provide stimulation.

Separating twins

Around one-third of twins are currently separated in school. Advice from Tamba and the Multiple Births Foundation says that the benefits of this can include:

- Multiples may want to be separated and their wishes should be recognised.
- If one child is markedly more able, either socially or academically, than the other, separation can reduce the risk of comparisons and competition between the two.
- Multiples may display disruptive behaviour when they're together.
- If the children are too dependent on each other and are not separated, they may find it hard to mix with and relate to other children.
- If they're in the same class, twins often strive to be the same, which can mean a more able twin under achieves, while the less able twin struggles to keep up.

- Twins, particularly if they're identical, can use their status to confuse teachers and entertain other children, but this can be distracting and disruptive.
- In boy and girl twins, the girl twin tends to develop faster and this can lead to 'mothering' behaviour, which may harm the boy's relationship with his peers.

If you decide to separate your twins, TAMBA offers the following tips to help prepare them to be apart at school:

- Discuss the separation with your twins.
- Take them on separate outings.
- Choose different pre-school sessions and activities.
- Take them on separate visits to their new school.
- Allow them to spend time apart with grandparents.
- Talk to teachers about allowing separated twins to have some contact during the day.

Delayed separation

If you choose to delay separation, it must be carefully timed to take place at a time when a change would occur anyway, otherwise one twin will remain with the same friends and teacher, while the other may feel rejected as he or she is separated into a new environment.

Never an easy decision, but one that should be made in the context of your children's individual needs.

Siblings

Older siblings of your twins, if you have them, can find the new additions to the family a challenge to get used to. On the one hand, they could get really involved in helping out with the twins and relish the new cherubs. On the other hand, they could find the attention they are used to getting hard to come by. Twins take a lot of time and effort and it is easy to neglect older siblings to some degree.

Make sure you give siblings time to spend with the twins themselves. You need to make time for the siblings, even if you feel pressured. Listen to their news with just as much interest as you used to.

Older siblings can be very useful when they and the twins are old enough. They can help at mealtimes, help get the twins dressed, play with them and so on.

You also need to contemplate ensuring older siblings have their own space, their own toys, to give them their own sense of individuality.

Space

You can never have enough space, I reckon, and twins don't do you any favours! It's never as easy as just buying yourself a bigger house, lottery winning excepted.

When they get old enough, it may not be possible to give your twins their own bedrooms, since rooms aren't ten-a-penny. If you can give them their own rooms, then they may well sleep better, find their own individuality and so on. However, if you can't afford them their own individual rooms, then giving them their own corner in their one room, or their own storage for clothes and toys will help them to develop their sense of self.

Whether it be their room, separate rooms or wherever they have been, teaching the children to clear up after them is essential. If they can do some of the work so that you don't have to, more power to them! Honestly, some effort teaching them cleanliness at the beginning will pay dividends later. You can develop games or songs to accompany the clearing, such as racing against each other and time, or a nonsense song about cleaning up, sung to a famous nursery rhyme.

At the end of the day, you might just have to be a little creative with the way you use space at home.

Holidays

If you thought taking your twins down the park was hard...

Holidays are something that some twin parents relish and others steer well clear of. It depends what tickles your fancy. My advice would be to work out why you want to go on holiday first. This then gets things into perspective. If you think you need a holiday to spend quality time with your missus relaxed on a sunny beach drinking cocktails, you might be in for a disappointment. It pays to be realistic, and quite often (particularly as your twins get older), the holidays are really for your children. Life is stressful enough with twins. Take that effort and move it to another country, with unfamiliar services and facilities, products and hotel arrangements, and you can see the challenges.

Matt and Karen's holiday case study

We flew early morning so we could give them some milk on take off so their ears didn't hurt - then they were asleep before the seatbelt sign went off and slept for most of the flight in both directions.

Travel with light hand luggage if possible as there are a lot of steps and buses to endure before you get on the plane, and with a buggy and two babies/toddlers it's not easy.

Think about what buggy you take - it might get damaged on the flight. Also, when you get there side-by-sides don't fit through most doorways and in lifts. We bought a cheap, narrow side-by-side stroller for the trip.

You can't sit together on flights with two infants even if you pay to pre-book your seats - there is usually only one extra infant oxygen mask per row.

We took rucksacks for them with portable DVD players in, stickers, crayons and loads of snacks and sweets - we didn't need it all but felt prepared for the delay at the airport and on the coach at the other end.

If you hire a car when you're away try to do this in advance and pre-book car seats. We found this was the easiest way to get around as getting on a bus with a double buggy would have been a hassle.

Consider staying in a family friendly resort the first time you take them abroad as it takes a lot of the stress

> out of it.
>
> It's definitely worth the effort to go abroad, we had a fantastic time - but try to go before they turn two as after that it gets expensive!
>
> Be prepared to walk or carry them a long way as you often don't get your buggy back 'til you've gone through passport control and get to baggage reclaim.

So clearly holidays can work, but you need to be realistic, work out what you want to get out of the holiday, and prepare. Equipment is vital.

Our fist holiday was in a campervan. We did not have a windshield to stake a protective garden around the van so the twins were crawling in opposite directions at a rate of knots towards various hazards. Oscar fell out of the campervan – quite a high fall – somersaulting into a faceplant. The boys had to sleep together and constantly crawled over each other, fell out of bed, and screamed through the night. Ostensibly, it was a disaster. However, with a little more forethought, and the correct equipment, we could have had a more successful trip.

Wrapping it up

So that brings us to the end of this little compendium of advice. I hope it has been in some way useful or reassuring. Remember, support and help is available when you know where.

And so what advice can I give you to round off this survival guide as you venture into the murky future of life with twins? Well, best leave that to Matt Bleakley of the Fareham and Gosport Twin Club:

Matt's Top 5 Useful Items for Newborn Twins:

1) ear defenders
2) whiskey
3) take away menus
4) dummies
5) more whiskey

Wise words indeed. Best of luck to you, and savour all the good times, remembering them for when you are stressed!

BIBLIOGRAPHY

Interesting facts and information on twins in the early part of the book:

http://www.multiplebirths.org.uk/media.asp (09/2010)

http://en.wikipedia.org/wiki/Twins (09/2010)

http://www.v-four.com/twinfacts.htm (09/2010)

Emma Mahoney (2003), *Double Trouble: Twins and How to Survive Them*, Thorsons

Dr Carol Cooper (2nd Ed; 2004), *Twins & Multiple Births: The essential parenting guide from pregnancy to adulthood*, Vermilion

Dr Marc Weissbluth (2010), *Healthy Sleep Habits, Happy Twins: A step-by-step programme for sleep-training your multiples*, Vermilion

Websites

For a great general baby website with lots of twin info too:

http://www.babycentre.co.uk/

Various twin organisations and websites delivering support and advice:

http://www.tamba.org.uk/